Wiley Global Finance is a market-leading provider of over 400 annual books, mobile applications, elearning products, workflow training tools, newsletters and websites for both professionals and consumers in institutional finance, trading, corporate accounting, exam preparation, investing, and performance management.

www.wileyglobalfinance.com

ADDITIONAL PRAISE FOR
THE FAMILY WEALTH SUSTAINABILITY TOOLKIT

"Fredda Herz Brown and Fran Lotery, who together have multiple decades of experience in providing excellent counsel to enterprising families, now bring us a new tool of assessment that can help a family to evaluate its potential for sustainability over generations. After you have read their book and used the assessment tool, I am sure your family will increase its knowledge of itself, and thereby your family's capacity to achieve its fifth generation in flourishing condition and go on from there."
—James E. Hughes, Jr., author of *Family Wealth, Keeping it in the Family* and *Family: The Compact Among Generations*

"This is an invaluable manual and tool for families that want to be deliberate about understanding, and then acting on, the opportunities and challenges of sustaining their legacies. The authors' reflections are honest and grounded in experience. Most importantly, the toolkit provides insights which empower its users to move forward."
—Christine K. Galloway, president and CEO, Okabena Company

"*The Family Wealth Sustainability Toolkit* provides an eminently practical framework for families to understand how to sustain themselves across generations. Fredda and Fran offer an opportunity for families to see that it's about more than just money!"
—Andrew Keyt, president, Family Business Network, North America; executive director, Family Business Center, Quilan School of Business, Loyola University Chicago

"The secret among most of America's successful families is that few have planned for sustainable wealth and lasting family relationships. This toolkit is the gold standard for anyone planning for their family's future. The families I advise can't afford not to read it and use it."
—Eric Kessler, founder and managing director, Arabella Advisors

"Herz Brown and Lotery have created a hands-on, practical book and tool for families who share assets to help them meet the hurdles that thwart most multi-generational families in their efforts to pursue their definition of longevity and success. The Toolkit will enhance a family's awareness of their family function, assist them in identifying opportunities, and aid them as they build a strategy for sustainability for generations to come. The manual not only provides a guide for families to understand sustainability, but also a way to make sense of the data they generate."
—Kirby Rosplock, PhD, fourth-generation family business owner and director, research and development, GenSpring Family Offices

The Family Wealth Sustainability Toolkit

Founded in 1807, John Wiley & Sons is the oldest independent publishing company in the United States. With offices in North America, Europe, Australia and Asia, Wiley is globally committed to developing and marketing print and electronic products and services for our customers' professional and personal knowledge and understanding.

The Wiley Finance series contains books written specifically for finance and investment professionals as well as sophisticated individual investors and their financial advisors. Book topics range from portfolio management to e-commerce, risk management, financial engineering, valuation and financial instrument analysis, as well as much more.

For a list of available titles, visit our website at www.WileyFinance.com.

The Family Wealth Sustainability Toolkit

The Manual

FREDDA HERZ BROWN
FRAN LOTERY

John Wiley & Sons, Inc.

Copyright © 2012 by Fredda Herz Brown and Fran Lotery. All rights reserved.

Published by John Wiley & Sons, Inc., Hoboken, New Jersey.
Published simultaneously in Canada.

No part of this publication may be reproduced, stored in a retrieval system, or transmitted in any form or by any means, electronic, mechanical, photocopying, recording, scanning, or otherwise, except as permitted under Section 107 or 108 of the 1976 United States Copyright Act, without either the prior written permission of the Publisher, or authorization through payment of the appropriate per-copy fee to the Copyright Clearance Center, Inc., 222 Rosewood Drive, Danvers, MA 01923, (978) 750-8400, fax (978) 646-8600, or on the Web at www.copyright.com. Requests to the Publisher for permission should be addressed to the Permissions Department, John Wiley & Sons, Inc., 111 River Street, Hoboken, NJ 07030, (201) 748-6011, fax (201) 748-6008, or online at http://www.wiley.com/go/permissions.

Limit of Liability/Disclaimer of Warranty: While the publisher and author have used their best efforts in preparing this book, they make no representations or warranties with respect to the accuracy or completeness of the contents of this book and specifically disclaim any implied warranties of merchantability or fitness for a particular purpose. No warranty may be created or extended by sales representatives or written sales materials. The advice and strategies contained herein may not be suitable for your situation. You should consult with a professional where appropriate. Neither the publisher nor author shall be liable for any loss of profit or any other commercial damages, including but not limited to special, incidental, consequential, or other damages.

For general information on our other products and services or for technical support, please contact our Customer Care Department within the United States at (800) 762-2974, outside the United States at (317) 572-3993, or fax (317) 572-4002.

Wiley also publishes its books in a variety of electronic formats. Some content that appears in print may not be available in electronic books. For more information about Wiley products, visit our web site at www.wiley.com.

Library of Congress Cataloging-in-Publication Data:

Brown, Fredda Herz.
   The family wealth sustainability toolkit / Fredda Herz Brown and Fran Lotery.
     p. cm. – (Wiley finance series)
   Includes index.
   ISBN 978-1-118-34586-3 (cloth/website); ISBN 978-1-118-42019-5 (ebk); ISBN 978-1-118-43190-0 (ebk); ISBN 978-1-118-41698-3 (ebk)
   1. Estate planning. 2. Families–Economic aspects. 3. Inheritance and succession. 4. Finance, Personal. 5. Wealth–Management. I. Lotery, Fran. II. Title.
   HG179.B74639 2012
   332.024'016–dc23
                                                          2012022696

Printed in the United States of America

10 9 8 7 6 5 4 3 2 1

Contents

Foreword   vii

Preface   ix

Acknowledgments   xi

CHAPTER 1
Achieving Sustainability: The Challenges, Opportunities, and Complexities of Enterprising Families   **1**
    The Business of the Enterprising Family   3
    Moving Toward Sustainability   19

CHAPTER 2
Family Legacy and Connection   **21**
    It's about Family, More Than Financial Assets   22
    Combining the Mindset of Shared Risk and Shared Opportunity with a Family Emotional System   22
    Family Connection: More Complex over Time   26
    Family Connection Independent of Sharing Assets   30

CHAPTER 3
Governance Structures and Processes: Helping Families Achieve Goals   **35**
    Family Mission: The Cornerstone of Governance   39
    The Shape of Governance: A Thoughtful, Inclusive Process   42

CHAPTER 4
Financial Accountability and Management   **49**
    The Individual's Role in Oversight   50
    Financial Responsibility across Generations   52
    Long-Term Management of Finances and Risk   56

CHAPTER 5
Human Capital and Leadership Development — **61**
How Does Human Capital Develop? — 62
Relationship-Based Competencies Are Most Valued — 63
Human Capital: People at Their Best — 69

CHAPTER 6
Roadmap to Sustainability — **75**
Designing Your Unique Roadmap — 77
About the Family Wealth Sustainability Index — 80
Results: Setting the Base Point for Creating the
  Family Roadmap — 82
The Roadmap to Sustainability: Planning the Future — 93

APPENDIX 1
Genogram Key — **95**

APPENDIX 2
The Samson Brothers Family Genograms — **97**

Index — **99**

Foreword

Twenty years ago, I founded a membership group focused on wealth management, but family issues are often what everyone wants to address first. Why? Because investing and wealth management for any family or individual is mired in, dependent on, and inextricably entwined with family dynamics! Over the years, hundreds of individuals have shared family secrets with me or confided in me about family conflicts.

Here's what I hear (more than once!):

> "Why do *our* family holidays together have to be spent listening to boring presentations by our financial advisers?!"
>
> "My sisters are totally uninterested in helping me oversee our family's substantial assets, and I feel isolated, set up to be the scapegoat if things go wrong."
>
> "Dad is convinced of his skill at managing our family's wealth by himself, and every day he seems more and more obstinate, if not irrational."
>
> "My family is far more responsible than my brother's, and I now can see that our equal share of the assets will end in disaster and conflict."
>
> "Mom is in denial about our wealth/Dad's dementia/my sister's spendthrift ways. How on earth can I get her to see reality?"
>
> "My brother's kids are being raised with totally wrong values because of his wife."
>
> "Why am I always the one my siblings ask to talk to Dad about thorny issues, like why none of them want any part of the family business. How on earth did I ever get roped into that?"
>
> "Our family leaves more unsaid than any family I know. If you think reading a book will help *us*, think again!"

This toolkit, part book and part online assessment tool, is different. In my role as founder of the Institute for Private Investors, I do not presume to help families solve family issues, but I do witness how families attempt to go about it. Seeking the help of an outside expert, many families express frustration with the jargon or touchy-feely style of too many "family consultants." Fredda Herz Brown and Fran Lotery have created an online assessment that allows family members to measure their values, future plans and goals contrasted with those of other family members to see where the family stands together—and just as importantly, where it may come up short. There is now a tangible and concrete way for families to see *exactly* where they differ; maybe the issue with Dad has nothing to do with his portfolio management and everything to do with his leadership style!

In addition to the online index, Fredda and Fran have created a book that acts as a companion for the tool, providing insight, a context and examples of their four dimensions of sustainability: Family Legacy and Connection; Governance Structure and Processes; Financial Accountability and Management; and Human Capital and Leadership Development. Throughout the book, Fredda and Fran weave a case study featuring a family tackling the familiar struggles any family can relate to, while also giving guidance on how the issues might be handled differently.

Advisers who work closely with families on their investments are too often frustrated by how family dynamics can derail the most brilliant advice the advisor has to offer. These advisors will find the toolkit of value in their work. Many families I know yearn to discover how they can maintain harmony while overseeing complex and significant assets. Many families I have come to know well fervently hope that the values and the care they have bestowed on their families will sustain the family today and for many generations in the future. These families will enjoy the practical steps provided here to meet that goal.

That is why this toolkit is so important—and overdue.

—Charlotte B. Beyer
Founder and CEO
Institute for Private Investors
Investor Education Collaborative

Preface

*S*ustainability as a concept came to us from our consulting work with multigenerational families. We had begun to think of the ideas of continuity and succession as inadequate to describe what we thought families were experiencing and what we were seeing in our work with them. The challenge for these families was not just how to pass on what they had in terms of financial or human capital. Rather, the challenge was more clearly how to utilize what was needed for the family now and leave not only enough to use in the future, but also to leave the knowledge, experience, and overall capabilities needed by the next.

In 2006, we made our first efforts at trying to more fully explore this concept with families. We developed a list of practices that we thought we observed in families that were most successful in sustaining themselves for more than three generations. We organized these practices into dimensions, and we developed a paper and pencil survey for families to consider. We not only used it with a number of client families, but we had willing colleagues examine each of the items in each of the dimensions to determine the content validity of each dimension and the face validity of each item vis-à-vis each dimension. With these data, we were able to begin to sort out what were good items and what were bad.

Surprisingly, we learned that one dimension we had included, philanthropy (or giving), was considered both by families and many colleagues to be a value statement on our part. We removed the dimension but felt strongly that the items be included, so we preserved them under the two dimensions of *family legacy and connection* and *human capital and leadership development*. We mention this because we want readers to understand that this tool was developed in a systematic and research-driven manner and because we believe that the tool itself will evolve over time—much like we believe the place of giving as an important dimension has evolved. We anticipate that with the continued use of the Family Wealth Sustainability Index we will not only further refine it but will also develop benchmarking data so that families can see themselves in relation to other families.

As we began to collect the actual data for the Index, we were also refining and elaborating the conceptual focus of sustainability. We began to use the model in our thinking about the kind of work families might do and included it as an organizing theme in our proposal writing for them.

In Chapter 1, "Achieving Sustainability," we define the characteristics of enterprising families that combine their emotional systems with their economic systems. We also begin to explore the concept of sustainability. Each of the next four chapters describes in detail one of the dimensions, which are: family legacy and connection, governance structures and processes, financial accountability and management, and human capital and leadership development. Throughout these chapters, the reader has the opportunity to meet, in a case study, the Samson Brothers family, whose members will demonstrate each of the dimensions. The reader will also have the opportunity to address some of the questions that the Samsons had to address as they evolved.

In the last chapter—Chapter 6, "The Roadmap to Sustainability"—the dimensions are brought together in a description of the Index. We instruct the reader about what the index does, and how to take and interpret it. The Samson Brothers family serves us once again by providing some initial data for us to analyze and then use to develop what the Sustainability Index is at its best—a way to provide a family with a roadmap to getting from where they are to where they want to be!

We hope that families and their advisors will find this tool to be useful as they strive to work with the complexities that are introduced when family and economy are woven together. We look forward to modifying the Index from your feedback and refining our model further.

Acknowledgments

No work of this size and depth becomes a reality without the help of a long list of people. While we believe that the acknowledgment of such effort deserves reward, there are no rewards that could measure the appreciation we feel for the thoughtfulness that others have applied to this project. Our worst fear is that we will forget to mention someone, not because of his or her contribution, but rather because of our memories! All of that being said, we are going to give this our best shot.

This work on the Sustainability Index was born out of our work with our clients. We were continuously trying to define what would contribute to their successes in family enterprise and to provide them with a way to see how they were doing. It was their initial interest in our work that inspired us to keep on going—from a paper and pencil tool to one that is more sophisticated and allows for comparative benchmarking data. The response of our clients has continued to provide inspiration, as we have gone back to them for ideas and for beta testing. We only hope that we can give back to them what they have given to us.

For those professional colleagues who offered us comments on both the content of the dimensions and the inclusiveness of the behavioral practices, we extend a big thank you. It is noteworthy that in such a competitive marketplace, we can count on a group of colleagues to help us develop "our" tool and that they are able to view it as an addition to their toolkits. There are so many, but to name a few who helped in many iterations: Jay Hughes, Charlotte Beyer, Patricia Angus, Sharna Goldseker, Scott Budge, Charlie Grace, Brian Hughes, Brad Fisher, Francois de Visscher, and Ellen Perry. We will always welcome your continued feedback as the tool goes live and is used by families. We invite the same from others as you use the tool and read the book. Its usefulness will come only as we provide data to assist other families and their advisors.

Our colleagues at Relative Solutions also deserve appreciation, for their emotional support and intellectual encouragement, and also for providing a forum in which to develop and expand these ideas. Dennis Jaffe and Sam Davis provided the forum for the initial expansion of these thoughts, and Carolyn Greenspon, Katie Dreghorn Linden, Ilene Weingarten, and most recently, Jeff Savlov, have provided for further expansion and testing of the ideas.

Karen Pursley, our office administrator and all-around "hold it/us together" person, provided the ever-present and diligent background work of our project. She has reviewed and redrafted several versions of each of the chapters and communicated with the IT people, led by Mike Tardif of Sourcetop, who also worked hard to meet deadlines and be creative at the same time. Marilyn Castaldo was very helpful in providing us with a way of getting started in examining our views on the subject and drafting some ideas for us.

Lastly, we would like to thank our families and our dear friends who put up with our incessant talk about sustainability and the project. They were giving of their encouragement and time all along the way and will probably be somewhat surprised by our availability as it reaches completion.

To all of these special people and to those we might have forgotten to mention—a heartfelt thank you!

The Family Wealth Sustainability Toolkit

CHAPTER 1

Achieving Sustainability: The Challenges, Opportunities, and Complexities of Enterprising Families

Families[1] who share assets—a business, a foundation, investments, and/or real estate—also share unique characteristics that tend to set them apart from other families. For these enterprising families, sharing assets adds complexity to their lives and demands significant decision-making and leadership skills, as well as some hard work.

At some point in time, a member or members of a family determined that they would share assets; that is, they would combine their family emotional system with a way of making a living, an economy. As a result, their financial and emotional well-beings are intertwined—perhaps for generations—and they must deal with the complexities of such a joining. Financially, they must make decisions together regarding how to manage what they have, as well as what they want to have. Additionally, there are subtle and not-so-subtle sets of decisions these families must make regarding how they want their shared assets to affect the emotional, social, and intellectual parts of their lives.

While family members can change their joint assets, those assets can also change them and how they relate to one another. For

---

[1] The family cases that we present are compilations of client situations from our work, but are fully disguised to protect confidentiality. In situations where the name is known and the story has been in the media, we draw on public data about well-known families.

example, their way of life requires enterprising family members to deal with each other around complex fiscal and business decisions long after they become adults. This demands an emotional attentiveness that sets them apart from many of their peers. Ultimately, if a family wants to increase its economic capital, it must work on its human capital—its emotional, social, and intellectual competencies. Although it may be challenging to keep economics from dominating emotional life and vice versa, sharing assets can provide an opportunity to develop family members who are financially and organizationally knowledgeable.

Our firm, Relative Solutions (www.relative-solutions.com), works with these families at the nexus of their economic and emotional processes, helping them address the challenges and opportunities they face by marrying the two. Through our work, we have come to believe that there is a way in which enterprising families are alike: For them, sustainability is key to their success. That is, the better able a family is to manage the business of the family, the more sustainable it will be.

While professionals in our field have assumed that sustainability means continuity, harmony, and togetherness over time, a better characterization comes from the definition for sustainable development of Earth as formulated by Gro Brundtland in the 1987 United Nations World Commission on Environment and Development (WCED) report, *Our Common Future*:

> "... *meets the needs of the present without compromising the ability of future generations to meet their own needs."*

The elegance of this definition lies in the fact that it addresses the need to leave enough for each generation to meet its needs without specifying how that might happen and without demanding sacrifice from today's generation. It also implies the necessity for family members to define the degree of connection with one another, their assets, and the world around them, both today and for generations to come.

Given the importance of sustainability for enterprising families, we have developed a Sustainability Index, an assessment tool that can help a family evaluate its potential for sustainability over generations. Used in conjunction with this book, the Index can serve as a sourcebook on sustainability for enterprising families—from those who own a family business, to those who own many assets of all kinds—and those who advise them.

If you flip to the back of this book, you will see you are entitled to one access code that will allow you to go online and take the Index, a series of questions that aim to assess you and your family's current appraisal of where you are on the path to sustainability. If you are reading a digital or e-book version of *The Family Wealth Sustainability Toolkit*, special instructions on how to access your code can also be found at the back.

Of course, the Index is only as strong as the number of family members who participate, so we encourage you to have as many family members as possible take the Index. More access codes can be purchased at www.wiley.com.

> This is how it works. Go to www.wiley.com/go/familywealthsustainability to activate your pin. If you are the first person to go through the activation process, you will be asked to register by creating a user profile and a unique family name. In order to benefit from other family members' viewpoints, there are three ways you can ask other family members to join.
>
> 1. You may personally invite other family members to join by providing the URL address above and the family name you created.
> 2. You may buy pins and request that the Index send out invitations on your behalf to other family members whose e-mail addresses you provide. Because the Index is inviting these family members on behalf of you and your family, they do not need to know the family name.
> 3. You may communicate the unique family name you created to family members who already possess a pin because they too own a copy of the Manual. These family members would also go to www.wiley.com/go/familywealthsustainability to activate their pin, create their user profile, and join a family index in progress.

THE BUSINESS OF THE ENTERPRISING FAMILY

One of the next-generation members of an enterprising family recently mused:

> Why can't we be like other families and just get together and have fun? Why do we have to get together to meet? That is the question I asked when I was younger, and now that I am older I can see why my parents and aunts and uncles thought it was important for all of us to be together at least once a year and spend some time learning about what our family does together; what my grandparents started and my parents and their siblings grew. It is really quite something. My cousins and my siblings and I get to work on some charitable projects with them, and in that way we learn about how our investments feed the foundation and how we can make a difference.

When asked how his experience compared with that of his friends he added:

> Since I go to a private school, many of the kids have a lot of money. Most of those who have fathers who work for some other company do not seem to do what we do as a family. My friends whose families own real estate or something else together, like a business, seem to feel more connected to what the family is doing. Some of them do meet together to discuss economic stuff and to learn stuff, but most of my friends don't understand.

We, and the families we serve, have come to believe that while it is most advantageous financially for an enterprising family to stay together as a unit—as it can then reap the benefits of a larger pool of assets to invest, as well as of an economy of costs—it may not be so advantageous on the personal or family side. There are potential costs of staying together, both for the family as a whole and, potentially, for the capabilities of the individual family members.

It may seem strange to say "the business of the enterprising family," since most of the family business advisors we know and some clients use the adjectives "business" and "enterprising" interchangeably before the word family. For us, enterprising families are those who commit themselves to managing—and in some instances, being creative with—the complexities of their system. They have developed a sustainable pathway to financial and family well-being. These families no longer tend to view themselves simply as the owners of a business, but rather as investors building a portfolio of assets that enhances all those who are stakeholders.

We believe it is critical to understand the uniqueness of these families in order to understand how best to sustain them. At its core, sustainability is a process of evolution, and these characteristics add an additional "burden" of planning for sustainability. When a family marries its economy to its emotional tasks, how does it balance the need for separateness and connectedness within and across generations? How well does it define the complexities of need versus want? And how does it handle the sophisticated decisions necessary when economy and emotion are intimately connected?

At heart, families who share an economy also share and must manage the following characteristics to become sustainable:

- They have a long-term, shared emotional history and extensive membership issues.
- They have tighter boundaries and struggle to maintain separateness amid strong family connectedness.
- Their family dynamics are more public than those of other families.
- They deal with complicated transitions.
- They have an increased tendency to triangulate and polarize in the face of issues and challenges.

As these characteristics provide the backdrop for developing a successful process for sustaining success from one generation to the next, we will explore them in more depth in the following sections.

A Long-Term Shared Emotional History

Like most families, enterprising families share a history and emotional connection that developed over time. They were families before they shared economic resources, and the notion of a business often evolved out of these families' emotional and economic needs. In order to understand a family's connections, it is important to understand its common emotional history.

Even nonfamily members who work in or with family companies relate to the shared history and connections that are at play in the work situation. These organizations frequently carry the family mission, vision, and values, which enterprising families often view as instrumental to their success. In fact, many work toward defining their culture and how they would like to express or implement it in their business, philanthropy, education, and investments.

The shared emotional history also provides a variety of important characteristics. For example, because family members know each other so well and have developed a shorthand for what they say, communication is usually quicker. Although this can cut the time necessary to work on something together, it also can prevent the family from fully examining how they make decisions and from hearing each person's view of a particular issue. The propensity toward "family think" tends to increase when family members are together.

Additionally, this shared emotional history often leads to patterns of interaction that come down through the generations and are often so ingrained that the family must work at identifying them.

> The James family enterprise was struggling with defining a joint sense of mission and purpose for the family firm started by their grandfather. The 18 cousins—2 of them worked in the business and 3 of them were leaders of the family investment company—were the offspring of 4 brothers and a sister who had a seemingly close relationship. When interviewed by the consultants, however, a number of the cousins expressed long-standing feelings of rivalry and being left out. Further, the children of the two oldest siblings were the only ones who were working in the businesses. The two older siblings were not fully aware of the rivalry until one day the cousins in one branch, citing their lack of interest and involvement, demanded to be bought out.

Clearly, while this family thought it was operating together, it did not understand that old family issues were impacting the way it viewed itself and how decisions might be made. We have found that families do well to examine patterns around four specific areas: How they exercise leadership; how they handle gender differences; how they deal with money, including making decisions about it; and how they handle power and control.

Achieving Sustainability

Drawing a three-generational family tree, or *genogram*, is helpful in getting families to see how their emotional history tends to play itself out in this context. We have a saying that *the past is always present*: What does not get resolved in the past, where the patterns begin, tends to be replayed. For example, a father who had an angry falling-out with his brother in business was vigilant about wanting his sons to get along when they worked together. But, his concern notwithstanding, they ended up arguing about the direction of the business and who would be in charge. Knowing past differences assists the family in understanding itself and in establishing governance structures and mechanisms that counterbalance the emotional tendencies.

Figure 1.1 is a picture of a genogram that we ask all enterprising families to complete. The boxes represent males; the circles represent females. Names and ages of each family member go in each circle or box. The horizontal line represents marriages, and the children from the marriage are listed in vertical lines joined to the marriage line of the parents, beginning with the oldest to the left. A double line through a marriage line indicates a divorce, and an X in a box or circle represents the death of the person. (See the Genogram Key in Appendix 1.) The genogram can also accommodate information about business roles and ownership of various family enterprises, such as using a double-lined circle or double-lined square to indicate that the family member is employed by the family enterprise.

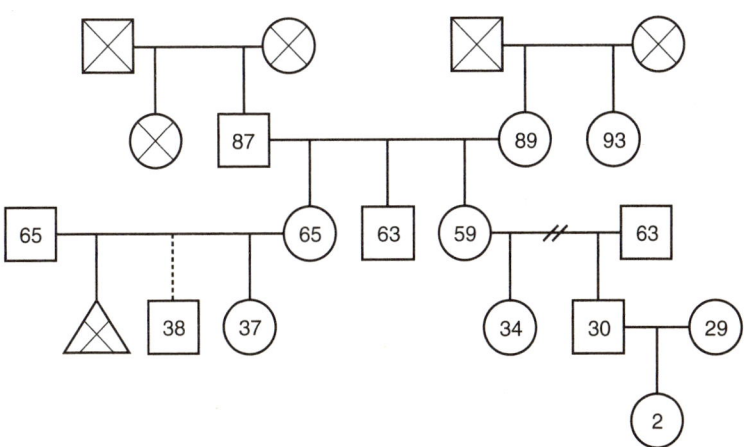

FIGURE 1.1 Sample Genogram

A genogram is like an evolutionary organizational chart of the family. Mapping the family's history and emotional connections for at least three generations permits one to see the patterns being repeated. By creating a family genogram of an enterprising family, the family relationships and the emotional connections between and across generations become clear. In the James family example, working with the cousins to examine how past sibling issues were affecting the current situation permitted the family to address these feelings directly rather than pull out of the enterprise. The genogram forms the backdrop for the family's archives, an essential aspect of the family's charter/constitution and its sustainability.

Tight Boundaries

All families have boundaries—both among family members and between the family and the outside world. These can be of varying intensity, but tight boundaries mean the family is focused internally and forms something of a closed system in terms of its relationships to the environment.

In our experience, the tendency to draw tight boundaries between one's family and others is stronger when there is a joint economic endeavor and a greater need to protect resources—literally and figuratively—from others. As one family described it, "our family name and reputation are so well known in the community that we are always struggling to keep something out of the conversation." Especially for those families who own a business that employs a great number of individuals or are prominent in a community for another reason, such as the family's philanthropy, being open to public view is like being in a fishbowl. Everyone thinks they can see in clearly, forgetting that the bowl itself distorts what is viewed.

> The Roberts family, now in the fourth generation, employed many members of the community in its three businesses. The family's legacy company allowed each generation to explore new areas of investment, and the Roberts were now not only in manufacturing, but also held extensive real estate. Everyone in the community knew about the family and who belonged to it.

> When the economic downturn hit in 2008, although the family would still be considered wealthy in most circles, they did not escape the effect of the recession. They were not prepared for the amount of scrutiny and public opinion that accompanied their need to back off of some long-term charitable commitments they had made. Additionally, one of their businesses was hurt badly by the downturn, and they had to lay off employees for the first time. The family found it difficult to accept the public view that family members themselves were not making a financial sacrifice, when in fact they were.

While tight boundaries can be protective, they may also tend to prevent a family from receiving accurate feedback on how it is doing or how it is perceived. Thus the Roberts family, described above, was surprised to learn from a close friend that others perceived them as having suffered little from the economic downturn. Our sense is that families who manage their boundaries well are those who are able to keep confidential and personal family information private while, at the same time, remaining open to appropriate input from outside.

A family that chooses to put its economic welfare together often runs counter to the prevailing norms of separateness. For example, unlike other families, in an enterprising family, young adults often do not leave home to make their own fortune. Instead, they must consciously define a self apart from the family while remaining part of the whole.

The lack of clarity between how separate and how connected they are expected to be to the family may hinder their learning opportunities and their social adjustment, and create confusion about how to set boundaries with people who want things from them. The family reputation may place undue burden on them in school, where they may question why people want to be their friends, or in the outside world, where they may feel they are being judged against the family performance overall. Friends may ask them for loans or expect them to pick up the tab for evenings out, though these junior family members may have limited funds of their own. If your family name appears on a campus building, expectations can run high among your friends. The family legacy, its heritage, brings enormous opportunity, but also many challenges. An enterprising family has to work at fostering an emotional maturity among its younger generation, giving them skills to deal with the specter of the legacy. Guidance to prepare younger family members is always a wise long-term investment. We will discuss this subject further when we examine human capital and leadership development.

One of our clients complained that having a family enterprise changed the nature of his relationship with his sons:

> I was speaking with one of the guys at the club the other day and felt quite jealous of what he described between himself and his son. He said that his children, now in their mid-20s, come home every few weekends to do their laundry and visit with him, sharing their career and job issues in a relaxed manner. Not so with my Ralph and Ed. I think it is because we work too much together.

Finally, a natural suspiciousness is not uncommon in many families, especially those sensing how everything that goes on within their boundaries is private. But in a family where economic survival may depend on privacy, a heightened suspiciousness of outsiders may lead to even tighter, more insulating boundaries. Part of this suspiciousness seems to arise from the perception that outside friendships might be based on what they have, rather than who they are. This fear of being hurt or "taken" fortifies the family boundaries, making it difficult at times for anyone to get in. Over time, with fewer opportunities to understand others' agendas, family members can sometimes become poor judges of people, permitting others to connect in ways that then exacerbate their suspiciousness and sense of isolation.

Extensive Membership Issues

For most people, marriage is the joining together of two people and two families. For families who share assets, however, marriage is the joining together of more than just families; the newlyweds negotiate the entrance of a new person to the family and its assets. That is, a person marrying into a family enterprise must figure out how to relate to the family and all of its holdings. For the Brown family this meant defining a prenuptial agreement for their children, which posed some interesting dilemmas:

> Gene Brown was 32 and getting married for the first time. He had been working at his career since college and had just completed his MBA. He met Olivia through his work, and they had been living together for a year, so she had the opportunity to get to know the family and all the relatives. Olivia came from an upper-middle-class family and was aware that Gene came from a family of greater financial means. She had always worked hard herself and was making an excellent income.
>
> Three months before the wedding, Gene's parents informed him that the family attorneys wanted Olivia to sign a prenuptial agreement so that the family assets would be protected. When Gene asked, "Protected from what?" he was told, "A potential divorce." For him, this was not a time to be thinking of divorce and worse, he had never told Olivia about the family's assets, which he did not even view as his. When his parents told him he must talk with her about it and suggested that the lawyer do it with them, Gene thought that was a good idea. When he told Olivia, she was taken aback; she felt as if she were being treated as a lesser person, being asked to meet entrance criteria to a family that did not trust her.

To avoid this kind of unwelcome surprise, it is important to treat a prenuptial as a joint effort involving both parties, rather than as a way to protect one or the other. It is also vital to provide a framework for young people joining the family so they understand how the family views the agreements around marriage. Beyond financial agreements, families must also consider guidelines regarding the participation of the new members and in-laws in the family meetings and joint businesses. Additionally, enterprising families may need to create a process to orient new members to their mission, vision, and values—just as they do for young family members as they come of age.

Increased membership challenges go beyond the time of entrance, however. As one family in-law reported:

> I came to my wife's family almost 20 years ago; we now have three children together who are almost at college age. I have had a successful career as a physician-researcher. I have very much enjoyed and learned from my involvement with the Grey clan [his wife's family] and feel very appreciative of what they have offered me over the years in terms of vacations and other kinds of trips and opportunities. My kids have been given great opportunities that I never had growing up, ones that I might have been able to provide for them. However, I am continuously struck by the fact that I have never been asked to share what I do with the family and have never been invited to share what my family heritage is about. Mind you, it is not that I feel like I am demeaned—more like unimportant. With so much involvement in my wife's family activities, I have little time to make visits to my family or to have my kids share that with me. My wife's family is all-consuming, and I find it difficult to explain my own family's economic means to my children who, of course, would rather go on great vacations than visit out West with my parents and siblings. It is a hard balance to strike, and I think my in-laws view the positives of what they offer without considering some of the challenges of marrying into this family.

The membership challenges were greatly magnified for this man and, unknowingly, for his wife's family. He had to figure out how to relate to the family beyond his relationship with his in-laws. Additionally, since many of the economic decisions he and his wife would make within their own marriage depended on the broader family, it was important to understand the details of that broader group. In fact, in this case, like others we know, the family had developed a set of guidelines and an introductory process to their family "assemblies," both for young family members joining for the first time and for people marrying in.

We refer to this process as an *orientation for new members* in an effort to invite them in. In the beginning, some families have assigned buddies to new members to answer questions and steer the new members to match their family involvement with their particular capabilities, interests, and availabilities. The first orientation meeting is devoted to reviewing the family governance and the family's educational and philanthropic programs or initiatives. There is also time put aside for new family members to introduce themselves to the family in a personal way.

Complicated Transitions

Because enterprising families are connected in so many ways, transitions in the family life cycle or business are fairly complicated and far-reaching. When we consider the potential ways in which families are stakeholders in any particular situation, we can truly understand the risks and opportunities associated with any transition.

For instance, the retirement of a senior leader in an enterprising family requires more planning than it would in most families. Retirement can signify a change in that person's perceived status in the family enterprise, and the family may need to reevaluate how it will move ahead with a potentially new leadership model and, possibly, a change in lifestyle.

Additionally, as we explained at the start of this section, getting married is a transition that is more complex in enterprising families, because family members and their new spouses must begin to relate differently, not only to each other and their families but also to the family's assets. Even if the marriage is between young people who come from similar backgrounds, and therefore may be more accustomed to how wealth and other assets affect their lives, their families may have completely different ways of relating to and dealing with their assets. They will still feel that, while everything is an opportunity, nothing seems easy.

Atypical and unexpected changes in family circumstances also raise simultaneous risk and opportunity for the family branches:

> Jane and her husband William were one of four branches involved in the family investments/office and philanthropy. None of the branch families had relied completely on the distributions from the investments for their income, and each family member had worked full-time. But William and Jane, like many of the
> *(continued)*

> other family members, had shared in a family personal medical policy, which they seldom used. When William was unexpectedly diagnosed with a terminal condition, they needed the insurance; they also were more reliant on the dividends/distributions from the family's investments for ongoing income. While the family could support such a need, it meant that there would have to be a change in policy affecting everyone. Something that would typically be the concern of a nuclear family (or perhaps branch family) became open to the rest of the family.

Similarly, for young people in enterprising families, making the transition to young adulthood is not without its trials and tribulations. As one wealthy heir observed:

> Making your own way in the world is hard when you come from a family that has some wealth. All of my friends talk about the other side, how lucky we are, and I don't want to seem spoiled or ungrateful. I know we are lucky, but I also feel it is tougher for me, at least in some ways. I have a father and grandfather and other relatives who are so successful that it is hard to find a way to measure how successful I can be—and what would constitute success anyway? When I applied for my first job, it was not clear to me whether I was being hired for what I brought to the table or for my family name and reputation. And to be honest, having extra money from distributions to do things is nice, but it also makes me feel like I am still a kid. How much do I have to make to be able to be an adult when there is always more?

This young man's father was also concerned about raising his children with wealth and creating conditions in which they could feel independent. He often remarked that he and his wife thought a great deal about how best to assist their children in managing the transition to full adulthood. Achieving a sense of independence is a task for any young person, but when money and the family are connected, the task is more difficult.

This is not uncommon in wealthy families. If these parents had it to do all over again, they would have advised against creating a trust for their son that paid out distributions beginning at such a young age. Had they known that the family success would have created such name recognition, they would have chosen a name other than their surname for their business enterprise and family foundation so as to be more anonymous, both in business and when making charitable gifts. In this family, the critical estate planning was created three generations ago to be tax efficient. This third-generation father wonders if his grandfather would have taken the same route if he had known that member of each successive generation would have to work so hard to become their own persons.

A Tendency to Triangulate

As previous sections note, patterns and issues tend to repeat themselves in all families. But, families who share assets have a larger platform for these issues and, therefore, more significant challenges regarding sharing, power, control, and decision making. There are clear opportunities in this situation, including a tremendous chance for family members to learn and relate to one another, both economically and emotionally. But the downside is that family members often become caught up in issues that don't necessarily involve them, which may lead to a situation in which old relationship alliances and grievances reassert themselves.

In fact, families can become polarized around issues. To an outsider with no previous knowledge of the family dynamics, it is easy to fall prey to these situations, unwittingly joining one side or the other. This is one of the main reasons that we, as a consulting group, tend not to agve to simply facilitate a family meeting. Each of us has had the experience of agreeing to do so and to present on a topic such as "developing a family council," only to discover at the meeting that the family has split into groups or sides, either supporting the idea or not, depending on whether they believe their family branch will receive adequate representation. Outsiders are viewed as taking sides, whether or not they intended to do so. For a consultant, it is like stepping into a minefield, which makes it hard to maneuver to help the family resolve its issues.

Triangulation helps explain these dynamics. At its most basic level, a triangle evolves when two people have feelings or differences about

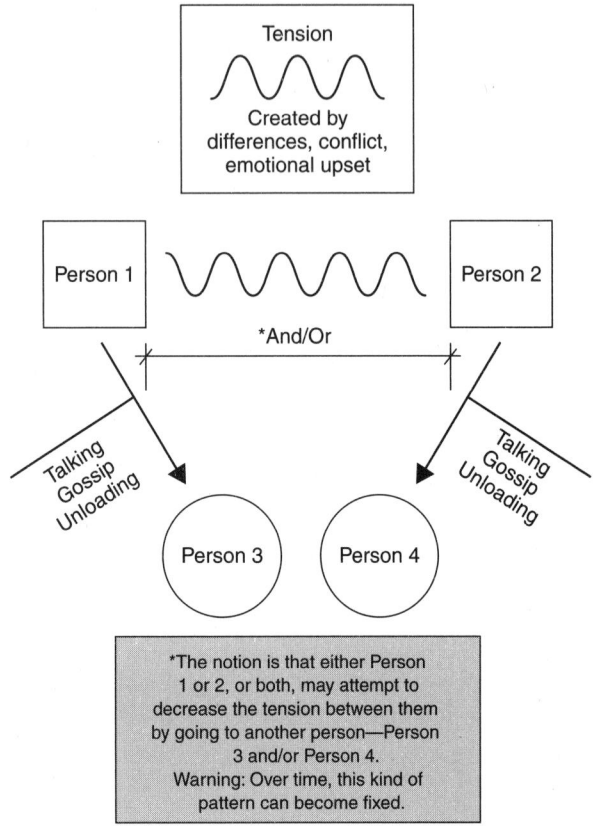

FIGURE 1.2 Triangulation

an issue, and, instead of talking directly to or resolving it with one another, one of them confides in a third family member. Having an alliance is often more powerful than being alone, but once the third person is drafted into the interaction, the second person does not know how the first one feels. (See Figure 1.2 for a possible illustration.)

For example, a brother-in-law tells his wife that he is upset at how his boss—who is also his father-in-law—treats him. She, in turn, confides in her mother, who talks to her husband, who wonders why his wife has taken his son-in-law's position in a disagreement about which she has no direct knowledge.

In triangulations such as this, family communication can become scrambled and complicated. Most important, the communication itself becomes a problem, as the two parties originally involved do not directly address the issue.

Triangles are basic to all human relationships but have particular intensity in relationships that are emotionally and, in this instance, also economically based. They generally consist of two insiders and an outsider, but they tend to be in constant motion, since being on the outside is not the preferred position. Thus, the person who feels like an outsider will look for a way to make an alliance with one of the insiders.

Triangles have generally been considered emotional processes, but their outcomes and perhaps intent can at times be political in terms of power and control. While family members and branches may move in and out of triangles with one another, over time the positions tend to become fixed, and when they do, it becomes more difficult to move into new positions. It is also true that individual family employees or advisors who try to align with some portion of the family to the exclusion of the others usually suffer in their ability to work with the whole family. At the same time, the family suffers, as it can't focus on resolving its issues.

One consultant faced just this issue:

> Larry has served as a family office professional for the Carne family for the last 10 years and has grown to understand the ins and outs of the family. He formed his own view and believes that one of the brothers, now in his 80s, is the most difficult one and causes most of the difficulties with the other siblings. Larry has aligned himself with the majority of the other family members in this view of the brother and, while he does speak to that brother and his family, his attitude toward them has not been the same as his attitude toward the others. He did not realize that the next generation had witnessed this alignment and has decided Larry could not serve them anymore.

"Public" Family Dynamics

From the earliest days, parents teach their children what is private and what is public information about their personal lives. And while the Internet may challenge these boundaries, most people still have a sense that their families are their private domain and that the dynamics—the interactions that play out therein—are also private, unless one chooses to share them.

But if you own a business, your family dynamics are more public. Everyone knows you and, in a small town, most of the population may work for you. Certainly, members of enterprising families are sought after for boards of directors, as potential investors, and so on. The truth is, the more these families allow the public to see them the more people will discuss them.

Indeed, our culture tends to be interested in and ambivalent about those who are successful, and, in our celebrity-driven culture, some people tend to think they have a right to know about others' lives. As a result, enterprising families often feel as if their lives are "public" in a way that others do not experience.

This young man describes his family's situation in such an environment:

> I was lucky. I grew up away from the family business and the community where it was housed. I actually never asked my parents directly, but I would guess that they moved us to a neighboring state so that we would not have to deal with living in the fishbowl my cousins did. For us, we were just one of a bunch of affluent kids, while for my cousins, everything they did, bad or good, was the subject of the town gossip or even newspaper articles. Since we were the town's biggest employer, my cousins felt pressure when business was in a downturn and always felt the eyes of their neighbors watching what they could afford. My cousin told me once that even my uncles' fights became something that was discussed at his best buddy's dinner table when he was there—with his friend's family showing a good deal of interest in their relationship.

While the importance of relationships across the branches of most families varies, in families that share assets, the relationships between and among family branches can take on a heightened level of observance and importance. Family history, too, which is often private in other families, tends to play itself out more publicly, with past relationship issues visited again in other generations. Thus, as was true in

Achieving Sustainability

the previous example, what was once an issue between siblings is revisited by outsiders and becomes a focus between branches and cousins. Perceived breaches and slights can work themselves into the family fabric, making their appearance unwittingly in leadership choices and decision making.

MOVING TOWARD SUSTAINABILITY

Ultimately, the unique characteristics of enterprising families create a backdrop for their lives and provide the basis for understanding some of the complexities that face them. Those families that understand the importance of sustainability recognize these complexities and accept that they will need to be thoughtful and focus on four distinct areas:

- Family Legacy and Connection—defining the connections among branches, developing community, and exploring social mission, values, and vision, for instance.
- Governance Structures and Processes—developing explicit structures, using genograms to map leadership and control issues, and building liquidity and exits for family members, for instance.
- Financial Management and Accountability—providing financial resources for the future, actively pursuing financial accountability, and determining risk management, for instance.
- Human Capital and Leadership Development—ensuring smooth transitions, developing the next generation, and making family members available as mentors, for instance.

These dimensions also form the basis of the online Family Wealth Sustainability Index that we discuss in detail in Chapter 6. Family members are asked questions within these four dimensions to best assess their family's strengths and weaknesses. Perhaps one family has terrific family legacy and connection but is lacking in financial management and accountability skills, and so on. The idea here is to provide a framework from which families can properly assess their strengths and weaknesses.

The next chapters explore these issues in depth, to help enterprising families navigate the challenges and opportunities of marrying emotional and economic concerns—and to ensure that their families remain sustainable over future generations.

CHAPTER 2
Family Legacy and Connection

Achieving sustainability is a journey, not an event. It evolves over time, with ongoing transitions in the family, and decisions made along the way. Achieving sustainability is complicated, but not just by the particular issues of any individual family; combining emotional and economic needs is *always* difficult. Shaping a family legacy that is formed in time, but not bound by it, is central to helping an enterprising family become sustainable.

Every family has a legacy, regardless of its economics: the heritage and traditions that are passed along, the values that are modeled, the DNA that is shared. Legacy has to do with the traditions, customs, and practices that are passed down, generation to generation. For a family that shares assets however, legacy can be more—it may also have to do with the inheritance and bequests regarding capital. Thus, for such a family, legacy also tells the story of how the family joined its emotional system to a financial one and how it became part of the foundation of people's interrelationships. While the family's composite of ingrained behaviors, values, and emotional connections has the ability to positively affect the enterprise's economic connections on a daily basis, it must also be monitored for its potential negative impact. While legacy may imply something passed in total, each generation has the ability to modify what is passed to the next, enhancing the positives so that by direction and vigilance, shared legacy can play its role in aiding sustainability.

In this chapter you will learn about:

- The importance of formulating a clear and compelling family direction or mission—a raison d'être
- How the family lore and culture define a family's philosophy of life and guides its members' conduct

- The tension created between separateness and connection
- Shared risk and opportunity
- Building trust and communication
- The benefits of a shared social mission

IT'S ABOUT FAMILY, MORE THAN FINANCIAL ASSETS

The family legacy becomes the culture of a family enterprise, which evolves and changes in step with the people who define it. Countless studies have shown that the most successful organizations have a strong yet adaptable culture—a character that participants understand, buy into, and take pride in. With families and with organizations, a culture doesn't just happen; it develops through management and nurturing, so that it becomes clear, compelling, demonstrated, accepted, and celebrated.

Having a shared family legacy is not as easy as it sounds. We believe there must be a conscious focus on the needs of the family and its individual members, integrated with the management of the financial assets. An Old English definition of *legacy*, "a group of people on a mission," certainly evokes the experience of a family that shares assets. Family legacy evolves into a philosophy that embodies both the direction of the family's holdings and the conduct of family members. Individuals come to see their values reflected in the enterprise. In the best of situations, the family legacy will inspire the group and help fulfill the individuals.

COMBINING THE MINDSET OF SHARED RISK AND SHARED OPPORTUNITY WITH A FAMILY EMOTIONAL SYSTEM

The stakeholders of the family enterprise essentially shape its legacy in an ongoing manner and use it as an investment in their future. While initially the godchild of the entrepreneur founder, it quickly becomes a part of the family's fabric. For long-term prosperity, investment is made through, on behalf of, and in (the development of) family members. Over time, family members share not only their vision, values, and hopefully, mission, but also some degree of risk and opportunity. Shared risk is a key characteristic of a family enterprise. Collectively and individually, family members are likely to be deliberative about family interactions—how they relate to each other in an economic sense, how they make decisions, who leads, how change occurs, and so on—all of which may influence their shared economic future, and perhaps, their emotional connectedness. Legacy involves how joint meaning is assigned to the shared economic and emotional life. It is how the family defines its beginnings and how it defines its future.

The patterns of family relationships, for instance, the dynamics, wittingly or unwittingly, are inherently part of the family legacy. They can vastly benefit a family enterprise, or also undermine it. But they are inextricably interrelated—the economy and the dynamics are bound together in the family lore.

When family members view themselves as being connected over the long-term, they tend to adopt a long-term perspective on their capital. Their focus turns to the future and determining the right balance of growth and value strategies. In addition to the long-term perspective on capital, there is also a need to keep investing in the future for continued growth through entrepreneurialism. Experience has shown that without this perspective and entrepreneurial spirit, a family enterprise cannot survive beyond the third generation. Often, the expansion of the family in numbers typically exceeds the increase of its assets, unless there is a focus on growth rather than just preservation. Not only is there an increased need for financial resources, but also for additional methods to keep the family connected as it grows in numbers, and for the diversity of its interests, values, and geography. It puts pressure on the clan to find ways to embrace this evolving diversity and find activities in which they can maintain their appreciation of one another, accept their differences, and cherish their family connection. Not only does a governance structure provide pathways for positive teamwork and effective decision making, it also is a way in which family members can get to know each other's capabilities and interests. Even though people may find a sense of belonging because of a shared legacy and family ties, long-term trust is built on experience.

If the goal is to have assets to pass on to future generations, and to remain connected to one another over time, then the family will want to be thorough in considering its intellectual, emotional, and financial capital, and the methods for using *all* types of capital effectively. The family governance permits family members to define how to organize and to manage the functions they choose to do together. Whatever structure is adopted, it can build in the processes for each generation to evaluate what it wants and needs from the enterprise.

In some families, the predominance of a past legacy inhibits change in the family and in its holdings. Family members are not permitted the freedom to be who they choose and have no ability to define their separateness from the family's collective definition of what it is. The tendency exists to hold on to a focus that is no longer viable for the business in the marketplace, since, as the following example shows, it may be viewed as part of the family legacy. A collective investor mindset can help in assessing the best use of assets. And a family governance process, which we will focus on in the next chapter, can help assure that strategic insights are surveyed and the right voices heard.

> A family enterprise that had operated in the United States for almost 75 years saw its market share in free fall, declining an average of 10 percent a year. Nearly everyone in the family was sharing in the business, drawing salary, dividends, or both. Despite the shift in marketplace demand, the elders in the group resisted change in business focus. Now generations three and four are grappling with how to keep the enterprise together and reinvent it for today's marketplace.

Shared opportunity is the opposite of risk, and the other side of thinking like an investor or projecting beyond the second- to third-generational transitions. Financial rewards are obviously a primary goal. But opportunities may well extend beyond economics, to allow for the personal and professional development of family members, providing experiences they might have obtained elsewhere in the external business world. An enterprising family is like a human laboratory for learning about a variety of subjects, including the economy, investments, decision making, governance, and leadership, to name a few. A family that focuses on how to provide experiences and education for family members can be a valuable source of legacy building as well as a way of generating business.

> One family developed an education committee whose task was not only to provide a way for the family members to learn about their legacy, but also to learn about the family and its holdings. The committee developed an orientation program for all new members of their family assembly. Then they offered regular courses on finances, developed an investment club, and initiated other opportunities for the family to learn from and experience working together. Each of the 30 family members from four generations participated in some part of the program with the next generation, eventually using their experiences in the program as part of the college and job application process.

One characteristic of participation described previously is its ability to foster continuity and legacy, as well as to encourage the development of individual and collective self-esteem. Family members participating in the enterprise derive a sense of self-worth from their contribution, whatever its scope. At both the macro and micro level in such families, the enterprise benefits when there is enough confidence to allow ingenuity and informed risk taking to flourish. This development of human capital within the family can reap enormous emotional and economic payoff for the enterprise.

A legacy is at once timeless and time bound. By the time a family business has been shaped into a family enterprise, the group understands that its legacy extends beyond the assets or property it owns, and a shared vision and set of values have been adopted. Each generation then has the important responsibility of molding its own vision and values, recommitting to the family legacy, and reshaping it for the future.

Adopting a shared social mission can sometimes be part of this process. A social mission often allows family members to see themselves as giving back to the larger community that has supported their success. The strongest family enterprises tend to encourage generosity and community involvement—whether local or larger-scale—in which their members can extend themselves and discover the personal reaffirmation that comes from contributing to the public good. The Rockefeller family is an example of a high-profile family enterprise known for its extraordinary good works. This sense of social mission and what it accomplishes can grow into a valuable bond among family members, enhancing their emotional connections and making them even more-effective partners in the business enterprise. A family's social mission can also serve as a learning experience, enlarging members' views beyond the limitations of their own self-interest.

FAMILY CONNECTION: MORE COMPLEX OVER TIME

Legacies tend to bring people together, just as sharing in the definition of a raison d'être does. We all know that strong bonds are the mark of high-performing teams—teams that people fight to belong to. And the more high-performing the team, the stronger the team bonds become as each builds on the other. Dramatic examples exist throughout the public and private sectors of the globe. As the saying goes, "One for all, and all for one." But sometimes these bonds can pull so tightly that as an individual, you feel as if you are being strangled. Feeling like you are your own person, a true individual, becomes a balance point. As with many matters related to enterprising families, it's complicated.

When families share assets, their individual members exist on a continuum that stretches between connectedness and separateness. On the one hand, the interpersonal relationships are the strength of the family—what holds it together long-term, rather than the shared assets. On the other hand, separateness or individuality is a natural human state and need. People are happiest when they can exercise personal choice. Employees at all levels perform best when they have some control over their work processes. And this applies similarly to those involved with a family enterprise.

Family connection balanced with the ability to be separate retains family strength and sustainability. Connection gains strength through flexibility. If members feel they have choices in the roles they can play within the enterprise, their commitment may increase. Alternatively, for those who feel stifled by family ties, separateness can become a cause. They may choose to pull away in smaller ways by diverting from family philanthropy, for example, or more dramatically, by filing legal suits demanding greater voice.

Sometimes this balance becomes critical for young people who may find it difficult to define their own mark in a world where much success is around them. Being able to feel free to pursue their dreams and to define what motivates them becomes important to their commitment to the larger family system.

> The Bells were a high-achieving family conscious of their status in the community. They had two children, both of whom were very accomplished. Liz studied dance and theater beginning at age four. She continued to be passionate about performing and had visions of becoming a choreographer and working on musicals.
> However, she felt compelled to follow in her father's footsteps and to attend his alma mater. He never told her directly that he wanted this, but Liz felt in her heart that he expected it. She did not feel strong enough to tell him she saw herself attending a performing arts program and working toward a career in theater. She loved her father, and did not want to seem ungrateful for the life he and her mother had provided her.
> So she majored in economics and after graduation went to law school. Although she continued to dance and perform, her studies were demanding, and by the time she graduated and accepted a job offer from a prestigious law firm, she had all but stopped pursuing her passion. Within the first year of being an associate, she knew she was in the wrong place. The only ones happy about her chosen career were her parents. She was conflicted about what to do. More and more, she avoided her parents and withdrew socially as well.
> Finally, at the age of 27, she worked up enough nerve to confess to her parents that she was living their dream, not hers, and that she hoped they would accept her decision to return to her first passion of performance. As it turned out, her parents were not pleased with her decision and wondered if she would be heading for a life of disappointment and economic struggle. They were also concerned that she would live off her inheritance rather than make her own way.
> Liz threw herself into dance and theater. She struggled for several years but was never happier. She did have some success, but not the economic success that she would have had as
> *(continued)*

> a lawyer. But she no longer avoided the family and took a great interest in the family's charitable giving. Through her influence, she was able to draw her family's attention to a project she was involved with that helped impoverished girls build self-esteem through theater arts. This project became a unifying family activity for many years, as it provided a way in which all the grandchildren could get involved in a community activity that was changing other people's lives.

As multiple generations become involved, connections increase in complexity. Each generation will evolve to its own dynamics, just as each must commit to continuing to share assets. Sometimes, as families move past the second generation, an interesting pattern begins to emerge: They naturally develop into a clan structure, with each branch forming a tribe that is independent, defined by its own geography, values, and structure, and yet part of the overall whole. A clan allows for separateness—discrete branches, separate households, broader definitions of membership and roles. At this stage, it becomes an increasing challenge in the opposite direction: How to promote connectedness of the clan as a whole in a united purpose, as well as in members of the next generation, who often did not grow up in one household.

As the clan grows, the pressures to keep connected and yet be separate, and to manage the system anxiety and tension, become more complex, and the opportunity for rivalries or inequalities to develop becomes greater. Triangulation—a form of indirect communication—becomes a risk: Polarization among individuals or family tribes and camps, can create destructive alliances that can be passed down from one generation to another. In our next topic, family governance systems and pathways for structured family communications, we provide methods for dealing with competing interests and other issues that have the potential to weaken the family enterprise.

Marriages, which are a cause for family celebration, are often a challenge to the balance of family connection. It is more difficult to deal with the introduction of new members in this way than through birth or adoption, since these individuals come with their own sense of who they are—they have their own values and culture. The arrival of new members at family occasions offers interesting potential flashpoints that are sometimes not sufficiently appreciated. Those who marry into a family may feel acceptance issues, whether or not they become a part of the enterprise. The process of integrating them may take time and effort. They may see their partners as "married" to the business, or the business as the central unifying force in the family. Others may see the family enterprise as a whole, not just the business, monopolizing their partners' time and attention. Some enterprising families set structures for entering or leaving the family enterprise, and suggest potential roles—formal or informal—for new husbands or wives in an effort to be inclusive; that is, to define the connections.

Even if a new spouse is not involved in the enterprise, tensions can arise. A strong family presence can sometimes overshadow appreciation of a spouse's achievements or reputation; or the enterprising family's demands may interfere with building effective connection to the in-law family that comes with the new spouse. How a newcomer is oriented to the family and the sensitivity of early interactions may want to be considered. For example:

> A researcher of some consequence married into the Grey family, who we introduced in Chapter 1. The Greys were an established family devoted to their business enterprise. In most settings, being a researcher would carry status. In this family, such success was not acknowledged. Over the course of 20 years, no one explored what the researcher was doing or asked how his work was going. The family's enterprise, its established connections, and its insular focus, all worked against appreciation of a new member. This left the researcher feeling neglected and inadequate, while also preventing the family from reaping the benefits of his contributions.

The explosion of social media since about 2005 has imposed new pressures on the younger generations. While enterprising families may wish to maintain a level of privacy about their economic and family activities, social media encourage open discussion about daily life, friends, and contacts. For younger family members, maintaining secrecy may be a social hardship and can run counter to the peer pressure they feel among their friends. At the same time, social media can also be an outlet for expressing points of view that are suppressed within the family setting. We believe that enhancing family communications at all levels is probably more critical now than ever. Without adequate avenues for younger voices to be heard, the enterprising family risks serious breaches.

FAMILY CONNECTION INDEPENDENT OF SHARING ASSETS

There comes a time in every family enterprise, usually by the third generation, when someone wants out of the shared asset pool. One or more members may feel sufficiently disengaged, or just have a need to be separate from the clan. Or perhaps they have a special need or want to pursue a venture independently of the family enterprise. Since we view the balance of separateness to connectedness as fundamental to these families, we believe that smart families enable members to sell their shares—without guilt—and still remain members of the family in good standing. Pruning the tree in terms of the family holdings when disinterest develops is important. Individuals should have the ability to withdraw from the economic participation, or then to rejoin if they change their minds. Either way, maintaining the emotional connection to the family is in everyone's interest. It's good business.

Clearly, family ownership is not the same as family membership. For some families it is viewed as an inheritance, in others as a gift, and still yet in others as something to buy. Each family defines how ownership is to be viewed, treated, and transferred to another generation. In this way ownership becomes part of the family legacy and shared value. Ownership issues that are not carefully defined and differentiated from family membership can be destructive to the family legacy. Accommodating for the changing needs of individuals is also an important part of the future focus that becomes incorporated into the family's legacy. The bottom line: Defining and continuing to build legacy needs attention every step along the way.

In the Samson Brothers Family case study, we introduce you to family members and follow them throughout the next four chapters. You have the opportunity to witness the family as it evolves over time and faces the challenges posed by each dimension on its path toward sustainability. In addition, you can participate in the family's

Family Legacy and Connection

evolvement by thinking about the questions posed at the end of each vignette.

CASE STUDY: The Samson Brothers Family (Genogram in Appendix 2a)

This first episode in the Samson Brothers Family case study provides history and context for the challenges the family faced for the future by examining the first dimension of family wealth sustainability: family legacy and connection.

Family Legacy and Connection Emmett and Conrad Samson are two siblings who bought their first rental apartment buildings in 1950 using their inheritance from their father, Carl, and a loan from their mother, Emma, for the down payment. They worked side-by-side until they eventually separated the apartment management and maintenance division from the development side. Samson Realty was a testament to their hard work and their working relationship.

Each was married, and between them, they had four children. Emmett married a local woman from a realty brokering business, Jennifer Lang. Conrad met Jennifer's friend Paula when she was invited for a family dinner. Not long afterward, they were also married, and the two families grew up together, living close by and raising their kids closely. Both wives felt a part of the business, including the initial decision to use the inheritance to buy the first buildings. Both couples felt it was important for their children to have a sense of connection to their cousins.

Education was important to the two families, and each of the five cousins were encouraged and supported while they pursued their college educations. Some even went further to pursue graduate or professional degrees. They all remained in close contact throughout, frequently traveling together and working together at their school breaks. The business was a frequent source of conversation at the dinner tables of both families.

In the late 1970s and into the 1980s, the next generation joined the family enterprise one by one as they finished their educations. Emmett's eldest daughter, Jane, who had worked summers in the real estate leasing division, had graduated from law school and served on the in-house legal team for a large family real estate company in another city. When she joined the family company three years later at her father and uncle's request, she worked with a long-term and loyal nonfamily executive, Bob Lanry, who headed the leasing area. Bob was asked to mentor Jane and assist her in developing the legal side of the leasing work. His plan was to retire in five years, leaving the department in her steady and capable hands.

As the eldest of Emmett's children, Jane was also the first to marry and, two years into her work with the family real estate company, she and Van were married. Van was an investment banker with strong ties to his family, who lived in another state. While he longed to move back to his home state, he also was very proud of the heritage of the Samson family. He thought that he could make a large contribution to the family enterprise by working with them on the funding and leveraging of their ventures, as well as by dealing with mortgages and tenant financial issues. Shortly after their marriage, Van asked his father-in-law if he could come to work at the company. Since there were few, if any, explicit rules for how to manage the next generation's entrance into the business, Emmett did what he always had done with decisions: He went to his brother Conrad and asked for his concurrence.

Conrad agreed, but thought in the back of his mind that this was just the beginning! They had both raised their children to be excited about and interested in the family business, and this would be the first of many requests to be a part of that business. In fact, he knew that his oldest son Dan, who was graduating from business school, would soon be asking for a job with the company as well. Thus, doing what he had always done, he agreed with Emmett's request regarding Van, in hopes that Emmett would return the favor in kind when he sought Dan's entrance to the firm.

Jane continued to grow in her capability in the leasing division; her father and uncle received great reports about the contributions she was making. Jane felt that she needed to be included in some of the "bigger picture" issues in the company regarding the expansion of the holdings and how it should be done. She heard a bit about this effort from Van but he, too, did not particularly feel that his contributions were well regarded by either Emmett or Conrad.

By 1978, Dan completed his MBA after receiving an undergraduate degree in architecture. He first worked for an urban planning company exploring issues related to creating mixed-use housing. After three years of building preplanned communities in urban areas, Dan was ready to see what he might do to assist the family real estate holdings. He approached his father, Conrad, to see if there were any opportunities there. Conrad reached out to his older brother, now almost 60 years old, to get his concurrence. Emmett was quick to say yes, not only because he always had liked and respected Dan, but also because he thought he had received acceptance of his children in kind. Dan began to work with Van on the funding and banking side of the business. Perhaps because of his background in architecture, Dan was always pointing out buildings he thought the family might find interesting from that perspective.

While the three next-generation family members, two cousins and one in-law, were joining the residential real estate management business, the business blossomed on the commercial side. Conrad, now 58 years old, continued to lead these development efforts. Conrad had a nose for the business and an eye for good real estate investments. He led the company into the New York commercial market in the early 1980s to take advantage of an economic downturn. Having always been very financially conservative, Samson Realty was positioned to take on some risk. The company was able to acquire commercial properties relatively inexpensively and limit their leverage during the high-interest-rate era. Van was instrumental in assisting the company in getting new mortgages, and in overall bank lending and deal making. He was quite respected by everyone with whom he dealt, and Conrad began to rely on Van's acumen.

Conrad's divorce in 1985 strained the company's financial condition because of the terms of the divorce agreement, which gave Paula a cash settlement and forced the sale of some valued properties. In addition, the financial hit seemed greater because there had been little planning with regard to either brother's estates and to the protection of current holdings.

Dan had begun to notice that there seemed to be little planning with regard to the ownership of buildings and had shared his concerns with Van. However, nothing was done and, consequently with the outflow of capital to settle the divorce, Samson Realty's ability to grow became somewhat limited. Growth through the 1990s slowed within the fairly new commercial area. However, growth was even more hampered on the residential side of the business because of the high percentage of rent-controlled apartments and limited funds to convert the properties to co-ops and condos.

The intra- and interfamily closeness also seemed to be impacted by Conrad and Paula's divorce. Jennifer and Paula, who had always been close, now struggled to maintain a relationship in the face of this new family reality. Conrad's children, Dan, Rachel, and his youngest, Peter, were quite angry about the situation, blaming their father for being inattentive to and distant from their mother. There was talk of Conrad being involved with another woman, a scenario he denied, and of experiencing a midlife crisis.

Conrad and Emmett's relationship seemed to be as solid as ever on the surface, but it was clear that the foundation had been rocked in some way. The next generation noticed that they did not spend as much time together and that their decision-making process seemed slower than before. In the family context, Emmett always seemed pulled between wanting to have his brother for family occasions while Jennifer wanted and missed her friend, Paula. And Emmett also missed her.

The next generation was increasingly aware that while there were changes in the relationships of the previous generation, their own families were growing. They knew that unless they began planning, it was unlikely that the business would provide the same opportunities for them or the future generations. Van and Jane now had two children, Billy (age four) and Rebecca (age two). Dan had recently married a young woman he met in graduate school. While they did not yet have children, his younger sister Rachel, who had married while he was in graduate school, had two children. Rachel and Jack (her husband) did not have an interest in the management of the company, but they clearly were going to be owners of the family holdings.

In addressing the following questions, think about yourself as part of the Samson family and consider the impact of your answer on the dimension of Family Legacy and Connection to assist you in thinking about the challenges and opportunities associated with it.

QUESTIONS FOR REFLECTION

1. How do you think the change in Conrad's marital situation impacts the cousins' planning?
2. In what ways does a change in marital status impact the legacy of the family and its enterprise?
3. While the previous generation had working siblings, the current generation has both working and nonworking siblings and cousins. What do you think changes in how family connections and the mission gets defined?

CHAPTER 3

Governance Structures and Processes: Helping Families Achieve Goals

Building a sustainable family enterprise is a special achievement that families share and can take pride in. Yes, it takes work and careful attention, but the payoff is tremendous. The bonds of connection and shared legacy lay the foundation, the roots for sustainability. Governance is the next step. It lends organization to nurture those roots, enabling them to flourish and adapt to changing conditions over time. Putting in place an effective structure to help organize family dynamics and decisions is a step most families aspiring to sustainability will eventually want to take.

In this chapter, you will learn about:

- Creating a representative governance structure that will enable the family enterprise to achieve its mission and goals
- How governance can resolve problems of trust and connection
- Formulating explicit and shared agreements about family assets
- The importance of defining liquidity and exit options for family members

Any family unit—even if not an enterprise—has some informal structure operating among its members, some implicit structure for making decisions. But for families that share assets, the need for a more formalized, explicit structure usually becomes obvious over time. Those who share assets will want a fair and orderly way to make decisions, consider opportunities, and deal with risks. Governance helps to manage the personal dynamics that can be both a strength and nemesis of a family enterprise.

In the early stages of being a shared family economy, an implicit hierarchy moves the enterprise forward. But once the enterprising family increases in size and complexity—for sure by the third generation, if not the second—more formal governance structures can be vital to keeping the family on track in achieving its goals. Often, the sooner these are put in place, the better it can be for all concerned.

Governance structures and processes assist families in managing what we have come to consider as five distinct, yet interrelated functions.

- Oversight of liquid assets; equity markets and bonds
- Oversight of illiquid assets; family owned and/or ownership stake in operating companies or real estate
- Family connection; developing relationships between family members, and having a shared sense of purpose
- Education; increasing the knowledge base and sense of stewardship and ownership among family members, learning to solve problems and resolving conflict, and developing leadership of family members specific to the needs and vision of the family enterprise
- Philanthropy; creating a sense of gratitude for being a recipient of the family's wealth, and learning about the needs of others and the act and meaning of "doing good" or giving.

There are certainly differences in the types of structures and complexity between the business-owning family and the family who has either sold their core family business or has evolved into more of a financial family that no longer shares an operating company, but shares a diverse portfolio of assets. The more complex the family and its holdings, the more defined the structures and processes will be to evolve and deal with them. Yet the functions to be handled are quite similar.

Formalizing the governance structure of even a small family—less than seven family members—also serves to help the family take on ownership and responsibility for the family financial, human, and social capital in a more orderly way. In this way the family can also codify their decision-making process—whether decisions are reached by consensus or some form of majority vote, and/or when certain decisions would be handled one way over the other.

At the same time, the family may establish specific guidelines for how often they will meet, what issues will be discussed, and what decisions will be made by which constituents. And family members can also address the differing needs of family shareholders for liquidity, loans, or other benefits. A group representative of the family (a family council and/or a family assembly) can also evolve, delegating some of the family functions to standing committees, depending on the need, such as education and connection, investment, and philanthropy. Each time the family enterprise faces a transition and/or grows in numbers and complexity, their governance structures will need to be revisited and changed to meet the changing needs of the family.

Families who sustain themselves for five, six, or more generations have usually moved to a complex governance that enhances the most positive qualities of the building of family wealth while balancing the negatives.

Why is there a need to develop this kind of family infrastructure? Because the bigger and more complex the family becomes, the greater the potential is for differences to arise among its members and what they want from the enterprise. Family members at different life stages, or with different approaches to money, may want to invest money differently. Some may wish to seek new businesses to invest in to employ their family talent, while others may want to play a more passive role and have a lower risk portfolio.

A family that hopes to sustain its economic base must be able to accommodate the diverse agendas, needs, and wants of future generations as it makes decisions in the present. Younger individuals may be involved with child raising and wish to use moneys to fund current lifestyle wants, or extended educational needs. They may want to undertake exploratory business ventures apart from the family enterprise. Elder family members may prefer to defer risk and increase the preservation of their wealth. Just as investment goals evolve from one decade to another during a lifetime, generations may have longer or shorter horizons in mind. Differing values toward money can also arise as a family increases in size and its branches are no longer as geographically close or experientially similar.

During the first and second generations of the enterprise, when family is still defined by those who grew up in a house together, it can seem easier to define what (and how) assets or wealth will be shared. But by the third generation, the family ownership group has probably grown much larger. Because people are from different families and may have different stakes, differing agendas may become entrenched. Siblings may have different numbers of offspring—an only child versus four children—and thus share unequal stakes. Elders may have difficulty loosening the reins, or adjusting to expanding gender roles.

> One patriarch from a family had been in charge forever, doing things instinctively. He couldn't understand why it was important for the family dynamic to now formalize decision making and governance. In addition, he had difficulty dealing with the fact that his daughter—a female—was now running the business he had built from the ground up. Though they had always been extremely close, once the roles had shifted he simply didn't want to listen to or participate in more formal family governance sessions. It took time for him to appreciate the value that an orderly governance process contributed to managing an increasingly complex enterprise, and to accustom himself to his daughter's special skills in dealing with the new challenges.

By the third generation, the family is likely to be more dispersed, or have individuals with differing needs for assets. All may be owners, but some may take a more active interest in how the family wealth is thought about or used. Some may work in the enterprise as executives, managers, or employees; others may serve on the board, and so play a crucial role. Among those who are investors or owners, some may be spouses, cousins, more distant relatives, or nonfamily members. Generational roles change; transitions take place, and the family confronts the challenges of exchange of power.

Among enterprising families, there is also strength in numbers. The family's opportunities for economies of scale and volume of investable assets are significant. But the shared risks and challenges can derail a family enterprise when there are no processes or structures for dealing with competing agendas that result naturally from varied life stages or differing life paths. Instituting family governance measures ensures that economic and emotional bonds are managed productively and for the good of all. The structure allows for everyone to get a fair share of voice. Effective governance systems help steady the course and keep the enterprise on track.

FAMILY MISSION: THE CORNERSTONE OF GOVERNANCE

So, what is the track, the course the family has chosen? Attention to governance begins with revisiting a family's vision for itself and its mission. A family's strength can benefit enormously when members take time periodically to assess their reasons for being together, and to recommit to or redefine goals. Clarifying these goals anew gives them an opportunity to work together on planning and furthers the interpersonal understanding and relationship building needed for sustainability of the family enterprise. This can be especially important when transitions are taking place.

Transitions are exciting times. They infuse fresh perspectives, creative rethinking, and renewed energy—all factors that can take a family enterprise to a whole new dimension. The transition from the second generation to the third is a critical time for an enterprising family. The family is expanding in size; the next generation is likely to have values and views shaped by divergent experiences. The original thread of purpose that birthed the enterprise may have been achieved. Those coming into their own in the enterprise may not have the same foundation of connection with more distant relatives that helped to ground the enterprise originally. The family legacy may still be valued, but a varied interpretation of mission may be driving its newest leaders.

Adopting formal governance structures at that point can help ensure the survival of the family as an economic unit while also preserving relationships. It's valuable to remember that the emphasis in governance is on the family (not the assets). Organizational processes and structures help an ever-enlarging membership manage the extraordinary tensions and complexities that are inevitable among a group of people who are both economically and emotionally connected.

The first step in instituting structure is to examine the reason the family is together—its raison d'être for being together economically. Typically, a family establishes itself as an enterprise because of several ambitious, but achievable, goals. They may wish to foster or leverage family connections, or may want to establish a family legacy business that will last through generations and embody a family vision. They may want to increase their liquid assets, or mentor future generations, or embark on philanthropy. Whatever the original impetus, the weighting of these goals is certain to change over time.

At times of change, a family will want to evaluate whether earlier goals are still priorities—or have they perhaps been achieved? Reasons for joining together can change during a family's evolution. A family who shares assets is wise to consider whether its personal and collective goals are still served by staying together when a transition is under way. This may be an ideal time for members to stop and reassess what they hope to accomplish as a family. If the goals of the individuals continue to mirror what can typically be accomplished by a family enterprise, then they can confidently move forward. And the governance approach that a family ultimately adopts should be constructed to help them better their odds of achieving these goals.

> A fifth-generation enterprise family had just sold its original business. Family members felt unclear about where to focus their future endeavors, but they knew they wanted to work together in some way. A plan was mapped out that entailed about a year's work. Family members met in generational or branch groupings to discuss vision and mission, and to define what shape they thought a new enterprise should take, including operating companies, investments, and/or philanthropy. A kick-off educational seminar was held to update the entire family and bring all members into the discussion. Work groups were set up to explore initiatives defined at that first seminar. Other meetings followed. It took a full year of teamwork to ultimately redefine the family's core values, vision, and mission, and to shape a new strategic direction that they could all agree on.

Governance captures each family's uniqueness. The mission and vision, personal to each family, become the compass that steers the course for the enterprise. The values expressed in the mission are typically reflected in whatever governance structures are selected as a good fit to meet a family's needs.

Governance defines how the family wants to organize itself to achieve decision making and to efficiently and thoroughly encourage family members to participate. It comprises both structures and processes that guide how the family will achieve its mission and embody its values.

Governance structures—and one size does not necessarily fit all—give family enterprises the tools to bring order to their midst, allow diverse voices to be heard, and make informed decisions based on shared values. From a boundary perspective, governance structures allow family members to participate fully in the enterprise while still retaining their sense of separateness and choice, which as we saw in Chapter 1, is important to sustainability.

Family members have many factors to consider as they develop organizational processes right for the functions they want to achieve as a family. What level of organization do they need, based on the complexity and size of their family enterprise? How many family members will be involved and in what roles? How should criteria be set for family member participation? How often should they meet? How will decisions be made?

Governance structures can take many forms. As mentioned earlier in this chapter, no one system necessarily serves a family over time. Governance processes are evaluated periodically to assure that they meet the evolving needs of the family group. Every major transition in a family is likely to prompt a reexamination of the organizational system in place.

Once a family has defined their core values, vision, and mission, they can then decide on the entities they might need to accomplish them. These structures, as mentioned previously will be different depending where on a continuum the family enterprise falls—from owning one business to multiple businesses, to diversifying assets, to selling the family business and investing in the equity and bond markets, or to buying another operating business.

If they are a business-owning family, they may decide to form a family council on the family side and an advisory board or a board of directors to offer expertise to the family in running their business. If they are family with mainly liquid investments, they may decide to add an investment committee with clearly defined responsibilities and guidelines for how they will function, comprised of family members with some capability and expertise as well as some independent outsiders, to oversee the family's liquid assets. This committee will create guidelines based on the needs of the family shareholders to deal with risk, asset allocation, return, and liquidity.

No matter what the assets, these types of families have to decide what is necessary to educate family members about such topics as: family dynamics, the family's financial holdings, or basic investment education about stocks, bonds, and private equity, as well as family member rights and responsibilities related to legal vehicles such as trusts, private trust companies, and corporate governance.

THE SHAPE OF GOVERNANCE: A THOUGHTFUL, INCLUSIVE PROCESS

How a family approaches development of its self-governance can vary. Everyone who has to live with the decisions of the enterprise should be involved in making them. The net for participation should be cast wide and deep. While this may seem unwieldy, getting everyone on board during the development process can help forestall difficulties later on. The first step for most families and their advisors will be to define the values and mission for the enterprise. The right governance process for a family that shares assets will be one that enhances the best of the family's dynamics while counterbalancing its most negative ones.

This development phase of governance can engage a family for anywhere from 6 to 18 months. This may seem like a long time, but once completed, the plan is likely to truly reflect the family's values and their needs. Goals of the family and the importance members place on different functions for the enterprise are usually carefully weighed. The Family Wealth Sustainability Index was designed to assist families in establishing a baseline of where they are on their path to sustainability and where they believe they need to go to achieve it. The data collected by the Index can point the way to the type of governance structures and processes that are missing and can suggest what structures and policies are needed. Such overall assessments take time and require dialogue within the family. A simple family meeting is not a setting for the deliberative process that needs to take place over months. Eventually, a family uses either voting or consensus to adopt a governance approach that is right for its particular enterprise and perhaps no other.

A key element in developing a governance structure for a family enterprise is allowing divergent voices to be heard. Building trust within a family enterprise is crucial. Many challenges can result from what is not discussed. The very process of working together on governance and resolving challenges can be a constructive way to share achievement and build trust. But families all have different tolerances for communication and transparency; each has to evolve to its own process and own structure.

> Within one broad, multigenerational family enterprise, management of all the major holdings had come to be handled by just one of six family branches. The other five branches were beneficiaries; none of their members worked in the enterprise, and they had no control. The challenge was to develop a governance structure that ceded control to one branch, yet also provided voice and participation for the others. Communication and transparency were critical to inspire confidence throughout the family branches. Avenues for frequent and two-way communication were developed and structured into the process. This took the form of developing an ownership/shareholder group that met independently to discuss their viewpoints on a variety of issues coming before them as owners. This group also periodically met with the board of directors of the family's holdings. As these two groups began to meet and understand the consequences of their current way of operating, the family members active in management and on the business board of directors began to see the importance of getting aligned with regard to the vision for their holdings. Otherwise, the beneficiaries would not understand why there might need to be a short-term cut in their distributions to invest in long-term growth.
>
> As a result of these meetings, there was eventually agreement that all branches should be able to qualify for the three family board seats and to participate in the selection process of independent board members. Over time, these changes served to increase the sense of the beneficiaries (those not in direct control) that in fact the managing branch of the family was not only doing a good job but also paying attention to the needs of the other branches. They also instituted a policy that encouraged internships and employment opportunities to all family members who qualified. Attention to building trust played a huge role in the family enterprise's eventual success.

A family constitution can be used to describe the formal governance process for how a family enterprise will function. Typically, this document describes how and when the family will assemble and how it will do its work. Committees are defined; membership criteria, and clear roles and responsibilities for family members are established.

Family meetings of different types will be defined, as will methods for ensuring that a smaller group of family members will be assigned to deal with family concerns between the larger meetings of the family. The relationship between the family and the business that it owns is clearly established so that the board and the family will be clear about the nature of their relationships. It can also contain articles that define liquidity and exit options. Opting-out opportunities allow family members to have more control over their own destiny and allow family members to remain family members even if they decide not to pool their assets. Understanding the conditions and pathways to obtain benefits, such as low interest loans to buy a house or seed a business, is another way in which family members feel more independent and in control rather than dependent. Often, just knowing it is a choice to stay connected to the family asset pool or to separate can deepen the commitment to the family enterprise.

A typical family enterprise works through the implementation of its governance processes over time, modifying them as needed. The ongoing goal is to cultivate among members an enlightened stewardship view toward the family wealth and to help the enterprise evolve from one generation to the other. Participation of family members is usually encouraged from an early age.

> The Jansens chose to invite their young people to join the family assembly at age 14 and become voting members with committee responsibilities at age 16. The young people went through an orientation held for new members, and, like others, were expected to attend family convocations once or twice each year. Advance preparation and active engagement were expected from all members at the meeting itself.
>
> Another family used a special session before full assembly membership focused on communication to educate its young people. Guidance was also provided in how to read the family's business reports, how to assure confidentiality in retaining the documents, and the care that needed to be taken in discussing family matters via social media. Bringing in third-party specialists to help in this process helped ease the internal family tensions and cross-generational pressures.

Governance Structures and Processes

Governance helps a family be nimble. When rapid decision making is needed, there is a ready process at hand, and that process is even-handed, with clear structures for communication. During difficult economic times, or when a major opportunity develops, a family forum can be pulled together for a reassessment and rebalancing of expectations.

Each generation finds the kind of structure and process that works best for it. The best governance structures really provide a process—a set of guidelines and protocols that helps a family manage the competing but interrelated interactions of its various constituent groups.

> The Green family had already experienced the transition between the second and third generation and was now anticipating the transition to the fourth generation. In preparation, they decided to revisit their existing mission, vision and values, and governance structure. Was it working? The family council decided to survey family perception by utilizing the Family Wealth Sustainability Index and found that for the most part the answer was yes. However, they also discovered that the next generation was not as connected to each other or the family legacy as previous generations because they were so removed from the original family business sold 20 years ago. Additionally, the family clan was increasingly more diverse and geographically dispersed. Concern was expressed that the family wealth would be taken for granted and that there might not be the energy, motivation, or sense of connection to grow wealth that existed in the third generation. Would the vision of the second and third generations to be sustainable continue to be realized if they did not actively pull together around a common vision?

The family council appointed a task force to work with the education committee to come up with a plan to engage the next generation. At the annual family meeting, with the help of a consultant, a series of sessions were set aside to bring the next generation together and engage them in a planning process that would assess what sustainability would look like in their generation and help them anticipate what they would need to do as future stewards and leaders. The second and third generations agreed to be open to changes and recommendations by the next generation.

Whatever form of governance is implemented, its structure can often serve as a valuable laboratory for both younger and elder generations, guiding them on how to work together and make effective decisions. Young people gain insight into the family values and business and develop leadership and management behaviors. Senior family members experience their family relationships on a new plane, playing different roles and stepping away from the traditional patriarch/benefactor interactions. Governance strives to organize the family agenda and gain full involvement of individuals in the family enterprise, helping to ensure their march toward sustainability.

You are invited to follow the Samson family as they meet the challenges of family governance.

CASE STUDY: The Samson Brothers Family (Genogram in Appendix 2b)

This second look at the Samson family examines how it coped with establishing governance structures as generations grew older, relationships changed, and the real estate economy fluctuated.

Family Governance   The Samson family was always receiving e-mails with invitations to conferences and workshops or with subscription offers to several publications dealing with family business challenges. Most of the family deleted these e-mails without reading them or after briefly scanning them. But Emmett, partly because of his concern about the growing complexity of the family enterprise and partly due to his tendency to find interest in those kinds of things, mentioned at a working family member meeting a seminar he saw advertised about setting up family offices as a diversification strategy. He said that he would like to attend with a member of the next generation. Dan, his nephew, said that he would really like to go, and they both agreed to report back to the working family after the seminar, thus ensuring that others might also learn.

About two months after they attended, Emmett and Dan excitedly reported to the family what they learned. While family offices were often set up after a liquidity event, many families had started them while they continued to own their companies. They discovered that these family offices were typically housed within the company office space (or as a division of it) with a specific percentage of the company income placed into a fund that the family would invest together. This provided a way for the family to diversify their financial interests and also introduced a potential way for the family to diversify resources for the human capital development of the family. Not only did the Samson family need more capital resources, but they also needed interesting entrepreneurial positions for other family members.

Coincidentally, Conrad's youngest child, Peter, was graduating from college with a major in finance. He was extremely interested in obtaining his CFP and CFA so that he could move into the investment arena. While no guarantees had been made to him, clearly this might be a way for not only Peter but also Dan and Van to expand their interests.

While the family all agreed that a family office was interesting, there seemed to be a bit of disagreement with regard to how to make the decision, the degree of risk they could tolerate, and the way the office would be handled. They went back and forth for several meetings with no clarity or resolution of the topic.

The second generation of working family members—Jane, Van, and Dan—decided that perhaps if they got together and came up with some ideas, they would have better success at reaching a decision. They realized that the family had grown larger with multiple interests at work and that the elder generation probably had less need and less risk tolerance for the family office even though agreeing about its usefulness. So they met twice, two hours each time, and hammered out what they thought might be a good plan that specified how much initial funding should go into the office and a methodology for taking it out of the company in a thoughtful budgetary manner. They suggested that the current CFO, Graham Foster, be asked to make room for the office in his portfolio of areas of oversight and that Dan begin working with him on the details of the area. All of the tax, insurance, and other documents would be handled through this area. The family would use this area as a way to invest together, increasing the amount available far beyond what any next-generation individual would be able to accomplish. The bill paying and other services that Conrad and Emmett used would now fall under this area as well.

They suggested that initial funding be in the neighborhood of $1 million, provided, if necessary, by leveraging one of the fully paid-for buildings. Thereafter, 5 percent of all profits would go into this area for investing. The three of them decided to run the idea by Graham to get his buy in before proposing it to the older generation. When they did, Graham became very excited about the prospects, not only for the family as a way to diversify, but also as a potential area of exciting and interesting prospects for him. With that endorsement, the three decided to present their plans to Conrad and Emmett.

At the next meeting of the working family members, Dan, Van, and Jane shared the overall idea for moving forward with the seniors. While it was met with a general positive regard, it was clear that there were many questions yet to be addressed. Emmett and Conrad wanted to know how Graham was going to handle the new area along with his current work at the company. How/who would make the investments? And how would they be involved as a family in the oversight of such, especially since not all of them understood investments? They wondered how, if the money was coming out of the business, the other nonworking family members could benefit from the investments? They were also unclear about how decisions would be made about the overall balancing of the family's assets.

They all had a sense that they were onto something that could be helpful, but they were concerned that without the appropriate attention to details, it might become another complication rather than a simplification of their holdings. Figuring out how to structure this vis-à-vis the family and the real estate company would be central. Also, setting up policies both to govern and educate everyone would prove helpful in the long run.

While they were considering all of these dilemmas, the family continued to grow; Ruth and Dan were now the parents of twin girls. Peter was getting closer to graduation and the real estate growth in New York City was increasingly being viewed as a bubble, potentially threatening the family's main source of wealth.

Bob Lanry retired in 1996, sensing that Jane was able to take over the leasing area. Jane and Van's kids were now teenagers demanding more of their parental interest and time.

In addressing the following questions, think about yourself as part of the Samson family and consider the impact of your answer on the dimension of Governance Structures and Processes to assist you in thinking about the challenges and opportunities associated with it.

QUESTIONS FOR REFLECTION

1. What policies and guidelines would you think the Samson family needs to assist in their decision making?
2. As they begin to think about diversification, what governance structure or structures might best fit the increasing family size and holdings?
3. How might they anticipate the future of their family holdings as the family moves to another generation?
4. In this first-to-second generation transition, is it time for the family to consider a board?
5. How confidently could you anticipate the future holdings of your own family?

CHAPTER 4
Financial Accountability and Management

It is generally expected that one mark of adulthood is the ability to be responsible and accountable for one's own financial resources. For enterprising families, in which the amount of financial resources is often significant, these resources are often complexly held and passed from one generation to another.

In this chapter you will learn about:

- Encouraging a sense of self-reliance, personal responsibility and accountability over the family economy
- How participation in family governance provides a laboratory for keeping family members in the loop and for building a sense of ownership
- Providing opportunities for family members to launch or sustain commercial interests that would support family wealth sustainability
- How philanthropy and investment clubs can be laboratories for developing the next generation

A family enterprise is also a shared family economy, where members are reliant on each other for successful management of finances. A powerful heritage unites them—a successful legacy business, a strong family web of connection, and a name with significance and equity in the community. The shared financial accountability for the enterprise strengthens the bonds and thrusts further responsibility onto family members.

The challenges of financial accountability can be daunting. How do they meet the current capital needs of family members while still assuring that there will be sufficient resources for future generations? How can they be certain there will be enough equity to go around without knowing the future? The recent upending of our economy is a stark reminder of how unpredictable our world can be, and how transient money is.

Gaining insight into their shared financial responsibilities can help a family shift from being one that simply owns a business to one that is concerned with return on investments (ROI). Preservation of wealth alone does not lead to sustainability. Families usually have to commit to a policy of *growing* their wealth or agree to settle for the alternative, namely, taking less and less over the years. The shared economy benefits when individual members see themselves as co-creators of wealth, embracing an entrepreneurial attitude that asks, "how can I contribute to the family's productivity and development?" Without this focus, family expansion can risk exceeding the growth of family assets.

Adopting a focus on the future is critical. Many factors are involved: spending rates of family members; how current spending rates affect the ability to provide for the next generation; what assets should be provided for the next generation; options for growing assets; considering when and how to diversify; and the difference between diversification and dividends. Those families who adopt this perspective are sure to become sustainable.

THE INDIVIDUAL'S ROLE IN OVERSIGHT

Every family needs a plan for regeneration of wealth that balances shareholder, beneficiary, and owners' needs for liquidity against what is needed for growth. And this plan works best when it has the knowledgeable commitment of every member of the family. Everyone needs to be paying attention.

The best hedge against risk can be knowledgeable, motivated family members who see themselves as accountable for management of the shared wealth. Accountability goes beyond stewardship to feeling a sense of ownership. Family members who have transitioned from feeling like participants to feeling like true owners are likely to exercise greater responsibility in their oversight of the enterprise. *Ownership* as a term implies to us more of a sense of active responsibility than *stewardship* does.

This sense of responsibility is generally modeled and encouraged across generations. Oversight is typically not assigned solely to outside managers and advisors. No matter how many outside managers a family has to assist them, families with high net worth who strive to be sustainable must retain oversight of their wealth. In order to do this, they will want to be sure they're getting the information they need, when they need it, and in a form that is understandable and accessible for their use.

Good information, communicated effectively, is crucial. Sometimes reports on financial assets can be difficult to interpret; for example, critical issues that need a response may be buried. Especially in a shared family economy, it's important for reports to be tailored to family usage. Documents should be easy for family members at diverse levels to scrutinize and understand, highlighting the vital facts and signaling opportunities or risks. At the same time, they must not be dumbed down and should require most family members to have a basic level of financial understanding. Over time, as families alter their financial structures, they may wish to adjust their companion communications, trying out different approaches.

> When the Johnson family formed a family limited liability corporation, government regulations required that the next generation be educated and involved. This change meant that the young people could no longer play a passive role. Regular meetings were scheduled; young people were expected to attend and be active. New reports were generated, and the younger family members were unprepared for the volume of information they now needed to digest in order to play a role in the new form of organization. They were surprised and unsure how to read and interpret all the new financial information coming their way. This helped engage the next generation in a meaningful learning process and involved the siblings in a shared project that set the stage for future initiatives in which they would work together.

Governance systems of the family can help with financial accountability. They formalize communication, assure outreach to all family members, and provide a structure for decision making. These factors build in an expectation of involvement, encouraging personal responsibility and a sense of ownership. The payoff will be worth it, if the organization can evolve to a fully engaged family enterprise.

FINANCIAL RESPONSIBILITY ACROSS GENERATIONS

Generational concerns are an important aspect of financial accountability and responsibility. The goal of sustainability has to be one that all generations buy into. On the one hand, sustainability focuses on the future and the youth of the family. On the other, it can be incumbent on elder family members to model appropriate values, such as understanding the balance between wants and actual needs.

It's valuable for families to start early, inculcating the concept of need versus want among future generations. Children benefit from being able to differentiate one from the other, in order to develop a sense of responsibility rather than entitlement. When entitlement begins to take root in a family enterprise, its effects can be enormously destructive.

So, how does a family go about instilling a sense of financial responsibility throughout its culture? By assuring that all members of the family are not only informed, but also appropriately and actively engaged in decisions regarding the finances of the enterprise. Members may participate actively in the governance or organizational meetings and structures the family has put in place. They may be afforded opportunities to contribute to developmentally appropriate decision making that will ultimately affect them and future generations within the enterprise.

> The Dade family decided that beginning at 12 years old, each of the next generation would participate in a financial camp in which they would learn in fun ways about money, budgeting, saving, and investing. The learning would continue throughout the year through their ongoing participation in an investment club where they would work with the older generation and the

> family office. In this way, once they turned 16 years old and were invited into the family business meetings, they would be able to understand the financial talk that would occur there. If not, they had a mentor (a family member) whose job it was to assist that learning process. The process moved from an individual sense of accountability to a collective one.

Sharing information and doing so transparently are also important. Educational messages get heard when they are age-appropriate and meet the interests of the listener. It helps to have a methodology, a process that specifies how and when youth of the family gain access to information or are invited to meetings. The family will want to factor in the impact of the digital age, too; today a young person can easily obtain public information on his or her family's wealth via the Internet. Too often, imagination about the size of assets can be greater than reality. It would seem better to obtain information directly from family members, who can dispel misconceptions and also provide some context. The question is not how great the family wealth is; the real richness comes in understanding the thinking behind how the family wealth is being thought about, used, and managed. Clearly, this is connected to how the family views its mission, a topic we discussed in Chapter 2.

Further, a family that shares assets will benefit its sustainability by trying to inspire, early on, a culture of entrepreneurship and productivity in its younger generations. While all members may not choose a business orientation in their adult lives, they need to be mined for their creative thinking and interest in the family legacy.

> The Flemings were fortunate in having built a highly successful family enterprise that was now extending to its fourth generation. Their daughters had been relatively uninvolved; they had chosen other careers and life paths. The parents wanted to encourage a sense of shared ownership. They sought their wealth advisors' counsel and brought in outside consultants to help
> *(continued)*

> work through some future planning and decisions. The girls' views were explored, and the family considered their interests. Over the next year, the daughters put into the works a plan for a philanthropic initiative and ultimately shared administrative control of a newly established family foundation.

On a very basic level, individuals need to be accountable for their personal finances first. From that develops a sense of accountability for the handling of joint assets. Especially with younger people, it can be effective to start them thinking about the micro view of their world and then develop that into an appreciation of the macro perspective for the family. At the same time, the more knowledgeable they become about the family assets and the more they see themselves as central to the maintenance of those assets, the sooner they will appreciate the need for their own accountability, and even personal budgeting.

High net-worth families have a convenient economic laboratory to offer their younger members. The youths have an opportunity to see how investments work, to hear how decisions about money are made, and to learn how to take measured risks. This protected environment can accommodate for their mistakes and provide valuable developmental learning opportunities.

> The grandfather in the Donahue family had been an avid investor his whole life and wanted to help his grandchildren appreciate the excitement of watching savings grow through smart investing. He set aside a pool of money as an investment club. The young people who began meeting with him at around 10 years old were coached and then given the freedom to choose their own stocks, make purchases, and follow the market, modifying their purchases as they chose. Their grandfather served as their coach providing guidance, questions, and facilitation. They learned an enormous amount from both the losses and the profits resulting from their choices.

Families often think that all assets have to be jointly owned. Sometimes, it's a case of agreeing on what is going to be jointly owned or on how a family handles what is going to be jointly owned. Family wealth may be divided into four buckets: one to spend, a second to save, a third to invest, and a fourth to give away. An important part of the learning process for any family is how to balance these buckets over the course of a lifetime. The personal bucket is the start—what it will take an individual and his or her family to sustain itself. The thinking needs to start with the individual and then move to a discussion among couples or the family branch; all this a preamble to considering the overall enterprise needs for sustainability in the present and for future generations.

Enterprising families may want to create policies or structures that promote self-determination and actualization rather than suggesting that reliance on inherited wealth is acceptable.

> In the Tuckerman family, the second generation showed scant interest in the family enterprise that had been established and was still being run by the original founding brothers. When the second generation realized that the financial benefits they were receiving would not be available to their children, they began to get concerned about whether the family resources were being utilized for maximum benefit of the members. They were concerned that financial support, such as education, and the pursuit of independent business interests that would potentially grow wealth, would dwindle. After going back and forth on alternative options, the two generations hit upon an approach that pleased them all: They would establish a family bank. The bank became an avenue for investment, satisfying current members, and also an opportunity for a family loan program that could launch or sustain the commercial interests of future generations. While this approach might appear to decrease current availability of financial resources, its effort was to increase the long-term wealth of the family by focusing on human capital development. This reallocation of resources clearly defines the use of assets in the current generation so that the next generations are able to meet their needs.

LONG-TERM MANAGEMENT OF FINANCES AND RISK

Financial accountability and responsibility represent risk management for the family that shares assets. Managing personal risk can be far easier than doing so for a large group of people. As a family grows in size, its risk appetite tends to change. Generations have different risk tolerances, and this can make for complicated portfolio management.

Over time, the family may come to require greater involvement by outside advisers and managers. This can be prompted by major changes in the enterprise, such as the selling of assets, an acquisition, the exiting of family members, or a transformation in business marketplace focus. Thoughtful use of outside specialists can add value and help to manage financial risks. But the effect of greater outside influence on family dynamics usually needs to be carefully monitored as well. Individual accountability of family members should still be maintained. The strength of the family enterprise relies on family members' continued sense of ownership responsibility.

Sometimes, trusts are established to protect the assets of younger family members. The appointment of outside trustees tends to separate individual interests from the family enterprise and remove some measure of control from the beneficiaries. It can also raise their risk, however, as control shifts to the trustees. Trustee relationships can be challenging, and each trustee and beneficiary relationship needs to be considered individually. Sometimes a family member is chosen as the trustee in order to contain all decision making within the family; in some situations, however, internal family dynamics can intrude on what may require the more objective perspective of an outside expert.

How the roles and responsibilities of outside trustees are defined is important. Families striving for sustainability will want to ensure that young people who are the beneficiaries of such trusts still retain responsibility for their wealth and play a central role in decisions regarding its use. In these instances, the trustee is viewed as someone who has the responsibility of working with the beneficiary to achieve financial accountability. In one family, the trustee met regularly with the young family members as they were maturing, acting both as a mentor but also mutually defining the nature of their relationship. In another family, the older generation was all too aware of the kind of parental and gatekeeper role that their own trustees had played with them and sought out individuals who would take their fiduciary responsibility to the parents' money seriously alongside their guiding role to the next generation. They asked the trustees to meet yearly with the next generation to review the terms of the trust (after they initially made their children aware of the trusts) and to discuss their children's financial needs and wants.

A family office is another construct adopted by some enterprising families as they expand in size and complexity. A family office can either be managed by a family member or an outside executive. This executive's role can be that of a financial or relationship manager who oversees budgets, manages trusts of family members, and helps effect economies of scale while also attending to the differing asset needs of individual family members. The hiring of the outside manager is likely to be a careful, shared decision within the family. The family will still retain responsibility and oversight and will manage the relationship with the outside manager.

> A fourth-generation family enterprise was considering whether the time had come to establish a person and place to handle the business of the family. Investments, insurance, and governance were becoming too significant a part of the workload for the family operational staff. Once the need for the family office had been clearly defined, a small task force was elected to develop the scope for the office and the job description for the manager. In this case, because no current family member met the criteria for the job, it was decided the family would seek a non-family manager. They gained family approval, hired a recruitment firm, and interviewed, selected, and trained the outside manager.

Having separate advisers is a way some individuals assure their interests are being represented within the family enterprise. Even when outside advisers are serving the entire family, they can present issues related to sustainability. It seems inevitable that over time they may develop more limited viewpoints or will develop alignments with some members of the family. Therefore, family leadership must be attentive to ensure that the best decisions for all continue to be the first priority for the joint enterprise.

Trust in one another is a part of the dynamic of the family enterprise. Their shared economy is dependent on the responsibility evidenced by individual family members. The trust that needs to develop among them will not be inherited; it will build over time. Making financial responsibility and accountability a core value within the family enterprise will help ensure sustainability of the empire they have so carefully built.

You are again invited to follow the Samson Brothers family as they meet the challenges of family financial management and accountability.

CASE STUDY: The Samson Brothers Family (Genogram in Appendix 2b)

This third episode of the Samson family case study examines how the family addressed the need for focused and accountable financial management to best serve the future generations' ability to sustain family wealth.

Financial Management and Accountability The senior Samson generation seemed to have had good estate planning advice and was not worried about their needs financially. They were interested in creating a joint family foundation since their advisor had suggested that it might be a way to involve their grandchildren in charitable activities, potentially increasing their sense of responsibility for others. Both Emmett and Conrad liked to remind their grandchildren that they were involved in charitable works from the beginning of their careers by providing affordable housing in addition to housing for the wealthy. They spoke to their children and their children's spouses, or in-law children, as they tended to call them, about their interest in pursuing this with the grandchildren and had received a good response.

Emmett and Conrad were most interested in how the next generations were going to maintain their wealth when there were so many more households that depended upon the family businesses to provide for their incomes. They were aware of the idea frequently called "shirt sleeves to shirt sleeves in three generations," which suggested that as a family grew, unless the second generation continued to work and add to the wealth, by the increasing membership alone, the family would be back to its origins by the third generation. They knew this was a game of numbers and did not want that to be the result for their families. They also knew that the next generation was struggling with the same dilemma and wanted to help them out.

Conrad grew elderly, however, and Emmett died. While Conrad appeared to still be in good health, he was increasingly frail. Conrad had remarried after divorcing Paula, and his wife, Margaret, about 15 years his junior, kept him occupied in travel and other leisure activities. He rarely came into the office and, when he did, he would come in, read the mail, talk with each of the kids if they were around, and then leave. On the other hand, during the previous few years, after Emmett had lost his wife Jennifer to cancer and seemed a bit lost without her, he grew closer to his children

Financial Accountability and Management

and spent a good deal of time visiting them when he was up north from his home in Palm Beach, Florida. His death felt sudden to his family, since he was pretty involved with them up to the end of his life.

With the third generation becoming older and greater in number and the number of family members and owners outside the business increasing, the Samson family began to think about how their wealth created significant new hurdles in terms of their knowledge base. While they were a family used to dealing with financial questions related to how to forge a real estate transaction, they were not as comfortable or as skilled in transactions that were investment-based in the equity or bond markets. They had expanded their diversification efforts and had come to rely on the family office to choose good investment managers but they felt increasingly outside of the loop on these endeavors. Even though transparency was not in question, they did not really understand the details that the family office president, their old company CFO, shared with them about this increasingly significant part of their lives.

Jane, however, had learned to understand the financials from the legal transactions she abided over in her position. Clearly Van, her husband, and Dan, her cousin, were most comfortable having had finance and investments at the core of their graduate educations. Peter had finally finished his CFA and was getting into the work of the business.

But there seemed to be a degree of tension whenever the family members who worked for company holdings discussed financial data with their siblings and cousins who were not in the businesses. Perhaps it was because the family outside the business just felt insecure with numbers, or assumed the ones inside had inside information on the investments. An increasing number of questions began to emerge addressing whether someone had "good" intent and whether certain people had the "right" to speak.

Non-family professionals began to notice when meeting with their family clients that some family members were unable to read the financial statements and couldn't capture a sense of what was happening to their holdings. Peter, now second-in-command of the family office, was beginning to worry about what would happen if this situation were to continue.

On a much broader level, the family governance that they had developed focused on the building of the family's wealth over time through the diversification of assets and liquidity options. It seemed there was no specific policy or structure in place, however, to deal with the family's challenges regarding ROI or risk tolerance. Continuing the discussions solely as family members seemed to encourage the disparity between the insider-versus-outsider mentality without intending to do so.

Each of the third-generation family members was acutely aware that their own children were being raised in a financial position different from what their own had been. They worried that the value of money had shifted in their families just by virtue of its availability. They were interested in what their father had suggested years ago with regard to teaching the younger generations about money management and accountability. By this time, their children ranged in age from just preadolescence to graduating college.

In addressing the following questions, think about yourself as part of the Samson family and consider the impact of your answer on the dimension of Financial Accountability and Management to assist you in thinking about the challenges and opportunities associated with it.

QUESTIONS FOR REFLECTION

1. How do you think the fourth-generation children might be taught financial knowledge so that they can fully participate in the family meetings?

2. Considering that the family enterprise can serve as a learning resource, what activities or projects might the family create to provide opportunities for the next generation to learn about governance and economic issues as well as family dynamics?

3. What are some of the obstacles, if any, generation three might expect as they involve the fourth generation in philanthropic activities?

4. What are some of the benefits, if any, that the family can gain by engaging the next generation in philanthropy?

5. As you think about your own family situation, what do you anticipate will be the most important financial knowledge to teach the next generation? Why?

CHAPTER 5

Human Capital and Leadership Development

Family wealth consists of more than just its financial wealth. As the saying goes, money is not what you make but what you make of it. It is the total of a family's well-being and the balance of its economic capital and its intellectual, emotional, and social capital (known as *human capital*). For families who have wedded their financial and emotional worlds, there are both increased risks and opportunities. Without acute and diligent attention to their human dimension, they further increase their risks and impede their financial prospects.

> *If you give a man a fish you feed him for a day. If you teach a man to fish you feed him for a lifetime.*
> —Chinese proverb

Human capital comprises the collectivity of what *each* family member brings to the whole. In developing human capital, a family strives to assure that each person has a concern for himself or herself, for others in the family, for the generations to come, and for social collectivity. How a family approaches development of its human capital can determine its long-term sustainability—enabling each generation to address its own needs while also equipping future generations to provide for themselves. When there is a commitment to the development of human capital, and it is viewed as an enduring value among family members who share assets, sustainability of the enterprise is virtually assured.

Human capital refers to the value each individual member brings to the whole family and is a reminder that the family is only as strong as its individual parts. It applies to every family member, whether working in the enterprise or not. For successful continuity as the family grows in size, it is important that all members, including those who may have married into the family, feel connected to the enterprise, regardless of the path they choose as they develop and follow their dreams.

We refer to the collective talents and capabilities of all family members as the assets in human capital. Encouraging individuals to aspire to their full potential benefits them *and* enhances the shared enterprise. Some families successfully build in exploratory experiences and learning opportunities to enable personal growth. Whatever form human capital development takes, it will want to respect the personal goals, achievements, and career interests of all family members. Strength comes from having everyone on board, understanding the mission and the vision of the family, and honoring the gift of ownership that each has been given. Families who successfully tap the resources of their human capital prosper both economically, through growth of assets, and emotionally, through successful family dynamics and communication.

HOW DOES HUMAN CAPITAL DEVELOP?

Relationships are the energy source fueling any family. For a family that has bonded its economic and emotional worlds, there is no turning down the heat on relationship attentiveness. If a family wants to increase its economic capital, it must work on the other side of the equation, its human capital—its emotional, social, and intellectual assets.

Leadership development is often a critical aspect of working with human capital in a family enterprise. Developing effective leaders among future generations is essential for sustainability. Over time, leaders of different types will take their place within the family enterprise. Entrusted by their relatives with special authority, they will face the pressure of both asset and relationship management. Our research on leadership in the family enterprise suggests that skills in solely technical and financial aspects of the business may not prepare them sufficiently for the challenges ahead.

A family will want to devote considerable attention to selecting and developing future leaders who are able to manage the complex interactions that arise when family members are also business partners. As the sizes of both the family and the nature of its wealth and its portfolio change over time, it is incumbent on the enterprise to ensure that current and next-generation leaders are equipped to handle the complex tasks at hand. The destiny of the family enterprise can depend on it.

RELATIONSHIP-BASED COMPETENCIES ARE MOST VALUED

"Leaders are made, they are not born," claimed celebrated football coach Vince Lombardi, and the business world has largely agreed with him over the years. Human-capital development has special import for a family enterprise because of the highly charged emotional connections involved between stakeholders. High-profile visibility in the external business world can intensify the pressure on families to effectively develop their next-generation leadership. It can be valuable to look at the experiences of other families when planning development initiatives for your own family members.

What personal and professional competencies should a family seek to develop in order to ensure longevity and prosperity of its enterprise? How can a family measure its effectiveness in developing its human capital and selecting its leadership? Considering such factors well in advance of major family transitions will allow for orderly succession planning and smooth change. Given their mutual accountability and concern for sustaining a legacy to benefit future generations, family members are wise to think about the criteria and competencies they may want to promote in their next-generation leaders. In recent history, when industries seem to have shorter lives and when the current jobs will often not be the jobs of the near or distant future, educating family members to be resilient, analytical, and emotionally intelligent become most important. In addition those who are comfortable in culturally divergent situations are also well served.

> For the Winters family, there had been three generations of young family members who had started to work in the family's electrical manufacturing company early in their careers. As corporate structure became more complex, the younger members were
> *(continued)*

> required not only to work outside the business but also, upon joining the firm, to serve in many different branches before joining the central office. These branches were in diverse locations and included one stint in a third-world country where the firm did some of its manufacturing. In addition, the next generation was now required to obtain some education in corporate and family governance. Learning about their own family history and patterns as well as their own role in the family dynamics seemed to increase the ability of young family members to lead with a strong sense of all their stakeholders.

Landmark new research is showing that relationship-based competencies may be among the most important for those who successfully lead family enterprises. In what may be the largest research pool surveyed among family enterprises, more than 550 individuals—working family members, nonworking family, peers, subordinates, and senior leaders—were queried using a 360-degree assessment process. This process, called the Family Enterprise Leadership System (FELS), was developed by our firm, Relative Solutions. The 550 raters evaluated the performance of more than 40 next-generation family members working in their family business. Their ratings of the most important competencies showed that factors related to emotional intelligence skills were more important than the organizational, business, or technical competencies traditionally used as leadership measures.

When using the Sustainability Index, you will be asked to rate whether your family has recognized and built into their behaviors a way to develop the next generation in these very important capabilities. When considering sustainability, these qualities and capabilities have become most central to preparing the next generation to be responsible stewards/owners, whether they are the family leaders or not.

These recent findings are consistent with emotional intelligence research conducted in the corporate world by Daniel Goleman, Richard Boyatzis, and Annie McKee, co-authors of *Primal Leadership: Realizing the Power of Emotional Intelligence*, a 2002 book that explains how to use your emotions, not just your thinking, in leading. Originally, in 1990, researchers Peter Salovey and John D. Mayer coined the term "EQ" to define this kind of competence and to serve as a measure of emotional and social intelligence.

In this FELS research among enterprising families, how an individual handled decision making was regarded as the most important competency. Further, how a leader reached out to other family members, communicated with them, engaged with them in making decisions, and delegated functions—these complex decision-making factors were seen as primary determinants of effectiveness by the FELS research. Careful observance of family legacy, family connections, and governance structure were seen to create an environment of mutual respect that fosters sustainability of the family enterprise. In fact, this makes perfect sense. Like it or not, human issues can make or break a family that shares assets. Human issues—family issues in particular—add unique complexity to the decision making in an enterprising family.

A family leader's results orientation and focus on enterprise vision and goals were also highly rated in the FELS research. A leader earned high marks by linking short-term actions with big-picture family interests, by adhering to family values, and by understanding his VIP customers, namely, fellow family members. Participants in an enterprising family have their lives invested there; they want to ensure that assets are being managed in accord with their needs, and that the equity in the family name is being enhanced.

A number of more traditional leadership measures surfaced in the research, for example, self-management and conflict management, but even these were interpreted in the context of a family's sharing of assets. Typical leader qualities of emotional intelligence—calm handling of challenges and success in managing personal impulses—were applauded. Self-interest was obviously *not* appreciated when family assets were in play. However, being aware of and managing the interests of all stakeholders was important.

> A founder's son, Joseph, had progressed through the ranks and was well on his way to running the family's furniture distributorship. However, several top salespeople and Joseph's younger siblings resisted the idea. He was often critical and sometimes became exasperated in executive meetings, appearing unprofessional and lacking leadership skills. At the same time, Joseph was frustrated by his father's lack of support and mentoring. Ongoing
> *(continued)*

> executive coaching was put in place for him, as well as a functional organizational structure, complete with job descriptions, responsibilities, and executive development plans. This helped to stabilize operations and calm discord.

Conflict surfacing in a family enterprise can be viewed in a positive manner. It can indicate that family members are engaged, accountable, and taking their responsibilities seriously. It also means that negotiation will be core to a family leader's role. Resolving conflicts can be challenging; a family leader needs to balance the interests of the whole against the needs of the individuals, allowing for all voices to be heard and proceeding knowledgeably and sensitively in managing the family dynamics. One way in which young family members can learn about each other and manage differences is to have opportunities to engage with their generational or age peers in joint activities. Philanthropic endeavors, which also build a collective and spiritual connection to others beyond the family, frequently serve well in this regard. Providing mentoring and guidance to these collective activities strengthens the intergenerational bonds of the family.

Family leaders cannot afford to abuse the status that comes with the role; they must come to understand the boundaries of when to act as an owner versus strictly managing the business. It is often wise to develop guidelines for all owner employees, since problems can arise at any level in the organization from, with, or between family members.

> As the Winters family began to define how they wanted to develop their young family members to work in their business, they also became more clear about the need to fully develop all members of their next generation, whether they served in the business or not. They believed that by doing so, all family members would develop an appreciation for the varied roles and responsibilities that go into being a family member with a collective responsibility. The family council, working with the company board of directors, developed the guidelines for a family member seeking employment and for career development of those who were

> employed. They viewed the monitoring and mentoring of employed family members to be the responsibility of both the company and the family. Family members wanting to serve long-term in the company would not only have to meet the job demands of their positions but also the requirements that come from being a working family member. These requirements were embodied in a document included in the family constitution called the "code of conduct for working family members" and defined the kinds of behaviors expected of family toward other family and nonfamily employees.

Leading a family enterprise is also a matter of attitude, conveying and fostering a sense of appreciation and gratitude for what others have made and continue to make possible by their efforts for each individual and for the family. Gratitude obviates entitlement. And cultivating it in family members is a subtle and worthwhile process.

> The ownership in a manufacturing company, with profits of $20 million, was transferred to three siblings, two sons and a daughter, when their father retired and moved west. The siblings and their spouses made all the decisions. At times, it seemed that very little could be accomplished because there was no forum for decision making and none of the siblings was a defined leader. However, the company had to grow because it now had three families to support. The families needed to define a business plan and diversification strategy and define the family leadership. They set up a new business structure, one that compartmentalized the company's sales and marketing, operations, finance and administration, and human resources. They also decided that within the company, the youngest sibling (a son) would serve as the president. This young man was not only extremely competent in finance and administration, but also seemed to have the best sense of how to manage the relationships between his siblings, the future generations, and the nonworking family members. Sales rose 20 percent, and diversification could then be considered.
>
> *(continued)*

> In addition, the siblings worked to clarify the rights and responsibilities of ownership, as well as the differences between ownership and running the company, and established a family council that began to develop a program for educating the next generation in relationship based capabilities. A board of directors was established, sibling conflicts were addressed at both the board and family council level, and the values and needs of the three separate families were discussed. In the end, both family relationships and the shared enterprise were considerably strengthened.

No one ever suggested that running a family enterprise was easy. It can actually be far more challenging than in businesses run by nonrelated executives and boards. In the latter, responsibility and authority are often viewed as more diffuse, and the enterprise is not linked with a single family name. Family leaders exist under a microscope, both internally and externally, in how they conduct themselves. Their decisions and actions are always scrutinized for, among other things, self-interest and family favoritism.

In addition, their performance tends to be seen as a reflection of the family. External visibility can always be a challenge for family enterprises, particularly if the family is a major presence in its hometown. Family leaders through generations eventually become accustomed to this scrutiny. They learn to manage it carefully because of its potential for impact on the enterprise, on family members, and on future generations for whom they hope to provide.

The representative governance model of family enterprises—where the legacy of the family and stakeholder ties run deep—puts special pressures on its leadership. One approach that serves as a wise reminder to the "leader within" model for individuals entrusted with family responsibility comes from the fourth-century-BC Chinese philosopher Lao Tzu, who said: *A leader is best when people barely know that he exists; when his work is done, they will all say, "we did this ourselves."*

In our contemporary times, this suggests that a leader's power can be defined in terms of how that leader exerts influence. The "best" leaders, reflecting on Lao Tzu's qualification, need to communicate the clear vision of their organization, understand their stakeholders, and be able to manage both their perception and their influence with them. In this way leadership is not based solely on defining policy but on igniting inspiration. Such individuals lead "from within" a family; leaders guiding members in the direction that the group has determined should be pursued while remaining true to their own principles.

HUMAN CAPITAL: PEOPLE AT THEIR BEST

When all is functioning well among a family's human capital, individuals will have an understanding of the shared mission and will identify with the value of the enterprise. They will be both engaged and inspired. And, whether working or nonworking members of the enterprise, they will feel empowered to seek personal fulfillment. Their richness as individuals will support the whole of the enterprise through times of transition, expansion, or marketplace change.

The strength derived from human capital doesn't just happen. Like all else in a family enterprise, it thrives with careful nurturing and attention. Each family that shares wealth will find its own way to foster enrichment of its human capital. For some members, participating in family governance can afford opportunities for continued growth and understanding as they take on defined roles and responsibilities. For others, family enterprise activities or shared community initiatives can enhance self-worth while providing insight into family values. A true family commitment to human capital development extends across generations, inspiring individuals to strive for their personal best and contributing to the good of the enterprise.

> A $50 million partnership was experiencing stagnation. Several attempts to encourage future leaders to initiate new ideas only resulted in lost profits, frustrated managers, and disappointed partners. A management retreat focusing on strengthening human capital was conducted for senior and middle managers, and partners. Here a strategic planning framework was introduced. Several participants working in different areas of practice had
> *(continued)*

> an opportunity to apply the framework to their own practice segments. Action steps resulted from this process, and follow-up on these by family managers has brought new energy to the organization.

Families that share assets sometimes underestimate how much mentoring, development, preparation, and understanding may be involved. Difficult conversations sometimes have to take place. Being explicit is critical within a family enterprise. Corporations have formal development plans; in families, these tend not to exist. "Leading by example" may not be a good role model for youths who go into a family enterprise and, in fact, they often should *not* aspire to act like "the" boss. Human capital development can help guide them to experience appropriate roles they can and wish to play. The Winters family decided that each of the young family members would have the opportunity to work in another country sometime during their high school or college education. It was important to the family guidelines that these learning experiences involve being part of a mixed group of young people in another culture. The Winters family council also designed a program for the next-generation cousins to work with one another in several philanthropic projects to increase their knowledge of each other, and their sense of what it takes to undertake serious financial decisions.

> Two brothers disagreed about the roles their children should play in their 25-year-old company. One of the brother's sons had joined the company five years ago and wanted an executive promotion. The other brother thought it was too early to promote him because he showed no signs of executive ability. There were no rules for family participation in the business and no plans for how to include the next generation.
> The brothers and their families were helped to explore and define exactly what the business meant to their family. Management, ownership, and family relationships were all considered. Over five generations, the family had operated several different

> sibling-owned companies that were never successfully integrated into a whole. Moving forward, this family established many formal parameters—job descriptions, performance evaluations, participation rules for its next generation—to more explicitly guide development of its human resources and human capital capabilities within the enterprise.

While sustainability of the enterprise needs to be a shared goal among the members of each generation, human capital development is all about the individual. The well-being of one family member can have enormous impact on the others. Their shared legacy bonds them, making it important to everyone that the capability of each person is well developed. The family benefits most when each individual is able to develop to his or her personal best.

Education plays an important role in sustaining family enterprises. The family enterprise can serve as a secure human laboratory providing extraordinary opportunities to see commerce at work, and to learn to earn, invest, and save. They can try out different jobs and behaviors and learn to take risks, make decisions, face challenges, and solve problems. Yet, young people in succeeding generations also need a mechanism for learning business lessons that employment experiences outside the family provide. Internships at the college age are a great way for young family members to learn the ropes within the family business, or even outside of it at other firms. Mentors within the family can contribute to their learning; senior generations have enormous wisdom to share, if they are available and committed to helping develop the family's capabilities while each individual pursues individual goals and dreams.

It is important not to underestimate the challenges and complications of becoming your own person when you are in a family that shares assets. Family and public expectations may run in a direction that a young person does not wish to follow. Defining your own passion in life and pursuing your own dream is a challenge. Enterprising families will want to provide ways for their younger-generation members to maintain their sense of family connection as they choose to pursue separate paths.

Ongoing human capital development, in the form of learning, as well as through participation in the family's activities and governance, is important for all generations and all levels within a family enterprise. Members' shared sense of legacy and connection benefits from continued renewal and communication. This will help inform their contribution to governance within the family organization, and their fulfillment of responsibilities for financial accountability and stewardship. The active participation of all family members, to whatever degree they choose, enables the enterprise to thrive and to fuel its sustainability over time.

You can now learn how the Samson Brothers dealt with the fourth dimension of sustaining family wealth, human capital, and leadership development.

CASE STUDY: The Samson Brothers Family (Genogram in Appendix 2c)

In this episode of the Samson Brothers Family case study, the third generation began to look ahead toward the leadership of future generations, and assess how best to employ the family's human capital.

Human Capital and Leadership Development While considering how to instill financial management and accountability in the next generation, the first cousins (Jane, Van, Dan, and Peter) began to focus more broadly on what the young people in the family might need to become responsible owners able to make decisions as stewards of their family wealth. Jane, Van, and Dan were clear that this was necessary regardless of whether the young people joined the firm or pursued other careers. They were also clear that they needed to provide a roadmap for the kids, vis-à-vis working in the business, including the rules for entrance and performance expectations.

Since they could not find a good way to decide who should be invited to explore these challenges with them, they decided to throw open an invitation to all of the children who were 15 years old or older, the age at which the family had already been inviting the kids to attend some of the family meetings. Much to their surprise, all of the next generation in that age range expressed interest and offered some dates that might be good for them to get together. The first cousins decided that Peter, the only cousin without children, would act as the third-generation representative to the group. They also thought that since he had no "horse in the race," he would be the most unbiased in his approach both to the notion of stewardship and to how family members enter the companies.

Peter facilitated the setting of the first meeting date, arranging for all of the second cousins to get together for about three hours to discuss their thoughts and concerns. While each of the cousins expressed varying interest in joining the companies as part of their careers, they were all most interested in learning more about the legacy and direction of the firm. They had varying degrees of understanding what the family business was about, but wanted to learn more about basic structures and how the company actually worked. Peter thought that was a great idea and suggested they begin a project of exploring, with their grandparents, both the history and legacy of the early business. They decided to split into teams to do the interviews and decided to tape them so that they would be available for the family archives.

When Peter reported back to his cousin and siblings regarding the tone and content of the meeting, they were delighted. Peter's commentary also pointed to some areas to keep their eyes on. Not atypically, Peter noted that each member of the next generation had different expectations with regard to what the business might provide for him or her. He thought it would be important over time to not only give them all a sense of what the business would offer, but also a sense that they should not depend on it for their support. He felt strongly that each of them should be encouraged to pursue a productive life doing something he or she felt passionate about. This led to an interesting discussion among them regarding the dissipation of financial wealth, what sustainability looked like for their family, and what it would take for future generations to be able to sustain themselves and eventually their families.

Ruth and Dan said that they had always provided everything for their children and expected them to do the same for their children. Jane and Van had a different viewpoint; while wanting their children to enjoy the finer things that they had learned to enjoy, they felt it was up to them how to achieve that goal for themselves. They said that they had begun their estate planning and were leaving a good deal of their assets to a foundation. While providing for their children in trusts, they believed that the money there should be used only for large purchases such as additional education, homes, and so forth. They had planned this way so that the kids, Billy and Rebecca, would view it as their responsibility to develop themselves, their passions, and their careers.

When Ruth and Dan asked if they had considered whether the kids' passions might not be remunerative in the fashion that Jane and Van anticipated, Jane and Van responded that they were willing to let that be and see what happened. To Peter, it seemed that the wealth that this generation had become accustomed to, as well as the differences in household values, might become a challenge for the family going forward. He suggested that his sister Rachel's family be included to broaden this as a family-wide initiative.

Along with a program for developing participation and leadership, Peter recommended they also consider discussing the ways in which each of the households viewed their wealth and what they had communicated to the next generation regarding their wealth. He thought his cousins also needed to discuss among themselves what they thought the next generation should understand about the families' collective holdings and their expected responsibilities: the kinds of educational and experience areas they needed to have in order to understand the businesses and their other holdings, the operations of the businesses, and the trusts that were established for each of them and for the collective group. Peter stressed that he thought the next generation needed some joint decision-making opportunities so that they could learn to work better together.

The cousins offered to work in joint work groups on these subjects with the next generation. Peter said he needed to think about whether such a configuration might impede the next generation taking responsibility for the work. He believed instead that the next generation having to work more on their own would assist them to do some thinking so they could truly have some dialogue with their parents about their ideas. While clearly he was not in a parenting role with the younger generation, he was not at all sure that he had the capabilities to facilitate the kinds of discussion that were necessary, or even, as the only single member of his generation, the attribution of leadership to do so. He agreed to think about the alternatives, get back to both groups for feedback, and then present his ideas about how to move forward.

In addressing the following questions, think about yourself as part of the Samson family and consider the impact of your answer on the dimension of Human Capital and Leadership Development to assist you in thinking about the challenges and opportunities associated with it.

QUESTIONS FOR REFLECTION

1. What practices are already in place that will increase the family's human capital?

2. How much agreement do you think there is within the cousins' group regarding what the next generation might expect with regard to financial wealth?

3. What challenges are the cousins likely to face as they put together a family mission/constitution?

4. What next steps would you suggest Peter take to deal with developing a stewardship program?

CHAPTER 6

Roadmap to Sustainability

In this chapter the dimensions of sustainability are brought alive in the form of the Family Wealth Sustainability Index, the online interactive tool that is part of the toolkit. It provides families with the ability to channel interest in sustainability into creating a family strategic pathway to getting there—a roadmap to sustainability. Remember, your free assessment code can be found at the back of this book, and you can access the Index by visiting www.wiley.com/go/familywealthsustainability. If you are reading a digital or e-book version of this book, you will also find special instructions on how to access your code at the end.

Achieving sustainability is much like a journey. An orderly route is plotted that accommodates stopovers along the way, yet identifies the final destination. Frequently, the need for alternate routes is taken into consideration and plotted out as well. Additionally, along the way, there might be some stumbling blocks that require a route revision or a detour. We hope the term *roadmap* suggests action—deliberately moving from one place to another to get you and your family from where they are now to where they want to go.

While the framework for sustainability has been demonstrated using a case study and other examples throughout this manual, the Family Wealth Sustainability Index actually connects this framework to family life. Each member of a family is actively engaged in the enterprising family's journey to achieve sustainability from the first moment of registration at login. This journey permits individual family members to first think about their experiences of how well their family is practicing the four dimensions of sustainability discussed in this book, and then to examine online the collective viewpoint of every other family member participant.

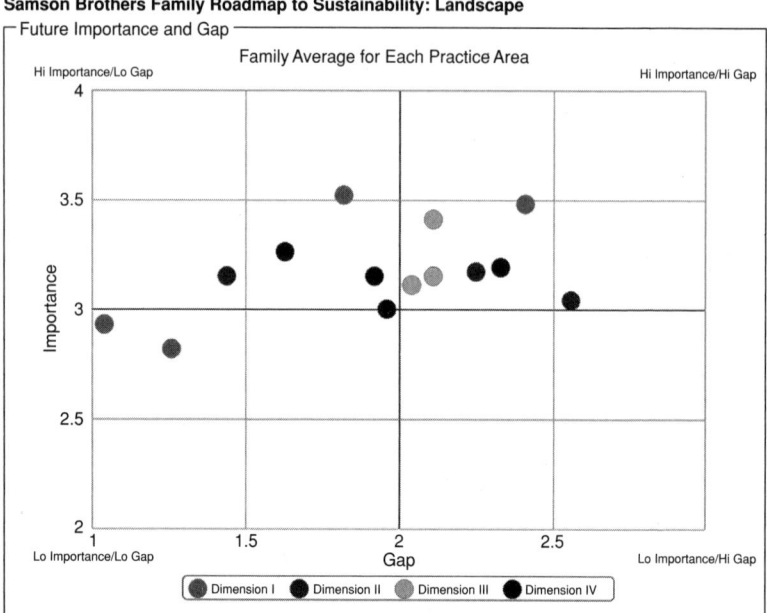

FIGURE 6.1 Roadmap to Sustainability: Landscape

Continuing the analogy of a journey equipped with a roadmap, the data collected from everyone in your family first sets a baseline or starting point where family members view the family to be at the present—at the start so to speak—and next, where you and everyone else want to go. In order to get to your destination, or endpoint—that is, achieving sustainability—the most important and necessary practice areas need to be attended to along the way. We refer to these moments as stopovers along the path. Finally, the best route is plotted—the most efficient way to get from your starting point to your endpoint. See Roadmap to Sustainability: Landscape (Figure 6.1) and Roadmap to Sustainability: Preferred Route (Table 6.1), both of which we come back to in greater detail later in this chapter.

Most journeys have a companion timeline—a way to plan or lay out how you will get from the starting point to the end point—describing the overall process. For instance when preparing for a road trip, there are certain things that need to be done way ahead of time, other things closer to the trip, and sometimes even during the trip

TABLE 6.1

Preferred Route	
Practice Area	Rank
Formulate a clear and compelling family direction (I)	3.12
Appreciate and enjoy extended family connection (I)	2.95
Develop paths for family communication (I)	2.93
Develop family's community and social mission (I)	2.92
Develop structures that enable the family to achieve its purpose (II)	2.87
Formulate explicit and shared agreements for family assets (II)	2.84
Define clear liquidity and exit options (II)	2.79
Maintain financial accountability (III)	2.73
Oversight of family financial management (III)	2.69
Provide for continuation of wealth in future generations (III)	2.63
Plan for leadership transition (IV)	2.61
Develop next generation leadership (IV)	2.45
Teach financial stewardship (IV)	2.18
Empower individuals to seek personal fulfillment (IV)	2.13

alternative routes must be chosen either out of necessity or choice. Attaining sustainability is no different. Figure 6.2 illustrates a process timeline in the form of what is referred to as the Roadmap Timetable (see next section, "Designing Your Unique Roadmap"). It is ongoing and fluid with times along the way to reflect, review, and revise quarterly, annually, and more long-term. It allows for moving back and forth along a continuum that is at one end more complex, and at the other more specific. Your family will establish its own Roadmap Timetable for its distinctive journey. It serves as a reminder that the journey is dynamic and fluid and needs ongoing attention in order for you to get where you want to go, rather than lose your way.

DESIGNING YOUR UNIQUE ROADMAP

This chapter will explain how to understand the Family Wealth Sustainability Index and use its results to create your unique Roadmap to Sustainability. Families that already have a structure in place for discussing issues and making decisions may feel comfortable meeting on their own. For those families that don't, however, it might be important to either call on a trusted advisor or engage a consultant to facilitate this and future discussions and planning sessions. The main

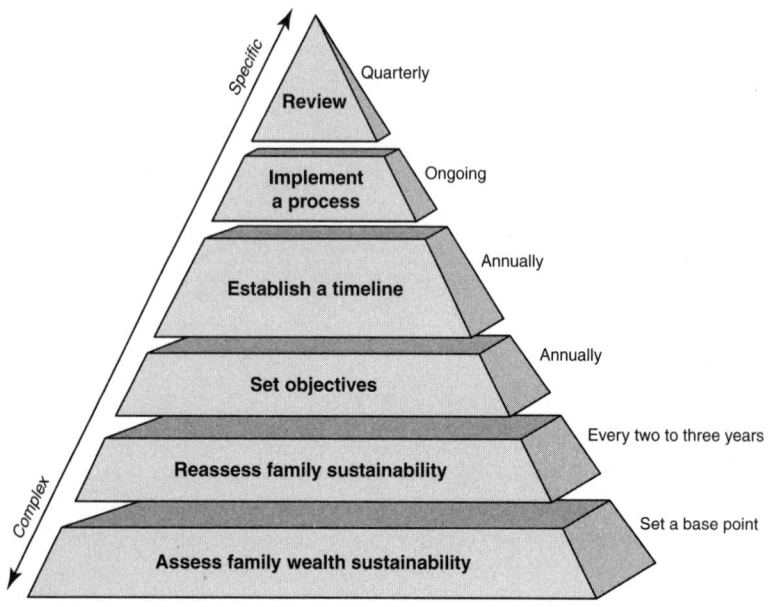

FIGURE 6.2 Roadmap Timetable

goal of these meetings is to understand the findings, agree to take the journey together, and develop the process (the timetable) for how your family will take the journey. While attaining sustainability is the endpoint, the process of getting there is vital. It is through this process that family members get engaged and take ownership of their desired destination. Together family members learn not only about what is possible, but also about each other, how to build trust, and how to identify who has special talents, capabilities, and leadership skill.

Throughout this book, you have been able to see how one multigenerational family, the Samson Brothers, has faced different challenges over time as their family and enterprise have grown and matured. These challenges have related to each of the four dimensions of the sustainability framework and have raised important and provocative questions. The example charts and tables used in this chapter to describe what can be learned from the Sustainability Index are derived from the nine members of the Samson Brothers family who participated. As you will see, these results helped this family to test out their assumptions about their future together by providing them with information as to their baseline, where to set their starting point and plot their stopovers, and by identifying the behavioral practices they need to master to ultimately formulate their family's unique roadmap to sustainability. As you find out more about the Samson Brothers family journey, you will also learn some ways to apply their process to effectively understand how to set your family's starting point and design your own roadmap.

The Samson Brothers Family case study describes one multigenerational family's development and evolution as a growing family enterprise.

CASE STUDY: The Samson Brothers Family

From the beginning days of Emmett and Conrad's sibling partnership through the maturing of a fourth generation, life has had its twists and turns—opportunities and challenges, both financially and emotionally. As the fourth generation was maturing, the family began to realize that financial accountability and management were essential skills to instill in a future generation that would come into wealth before they might earn it themselves. Additionally, as the family was considering diversifying its assets, the family office was becoming more formalized and starting to raise questions about how it would be overseen and how it would benefit family members not working in the current business.

As far back as when Conrad agreed with Emmett to allow Van, Jane's husband, to join the business, he recognized that there would be other requests from the third generation to have the opportunity to work in the family business. This prediction turned out to be true, as the fourth generation began asking about how it might also join the business.

Where to start? What family strategic pathway has the best fit given its goal of attaining family wealth sustainability? Do they continue to join their assets together or unbundle them? Is it an all-or-nothing decision or a both/and? What policies and structures will they need to help them execute whatever choice they make? How can they continue their shared legacy and connection?

When the Samsons were introduced to the sustainability framework, it aligned with their view of a desired future that, using the definition Gro Brundtland formulated in the 1987 UN report *Our Common Future*, "... meets the needs of the present without compromising the ability of future generations to meet their own needs." The Samsons knew their success depended on enlisting all three generations in designing their family's roadmap. The first cousins had already agreed that the fourth generation would need to be engaged and also educated about responsible ownership and stewardship of the family wealth. They also knew that they were going to need to formalize some policies, such as outlining the requirements for

(continued)

working in the family enterprise. The third-generation first cousins selected Peter as their generational representative to lead the charge and set their roadmap timetable in motion.

In Chapter 5, the Samson Brothers case ended with Peter briefing his cousins and siblings about his first meeting with the fourth generation. Soon after, one of the family's financial advisors introduced Peter to the Sustainability Index.

This is a typical point at which enterprising families begin to think about the future and how they would manage a growing family and multiple future owners of the family holdings. Having access to a tool that would assist them in plotting a beginning point and assessing what they, as a family, might need to do to attain the right level of sustainability made a lot of sense to them as the complexity of their family enterprise grew by numbers of people, assets, geographic distances, and different branch cultures.

Before looking at what results the tool provides and how to use it, let's digress a bit in order to gain an understanding of how the tool works, what happens at login, and then how to make sense of the two types of results it produces.

ABOUT THE FAMILY WEALTH SUSTAINABILITY INDEX

The Family Wealth Sustainability Index tool gathers information across four dimensions that define wealth sustainability. In this way, it bears similarity to an analysis employed by an organization to ferret out potential challenges, threats, and opportunities. The four dimensions are:

I. Family Legacy and Connection
II. Governance Structures and Processes
III. Financial Accountability and Management
IV. Human Capital and Leadership Development

Each of the four dimensions is composed of three or more general practice areas, which, in turn are defined by three or more behavioral practices. These practices might be thought of as "best practices" for sustainability, in that individuals who are considered to be experts in

TABLE 6.2

Rating Scale

	In the **CURRENT** column, click on a number button to indicate the degree to which you see your family using that practice now, using this 0-4 rating scale.		In the **FUTURE IMPORTANCE** column, click on a number button to indicate how important you consider that practice will be for your family in the near future (next five years), using this 0-4 rating scale.
0	Our family does not do this at all	0	This would not be important at all
1	Our family does this rarely	1	This would be slightly important
2	Our family does this some of the time	2	This would be moderately important
3	Our family does this most of the time	3	This would be solidly important
4	Our family does this as a regular practice	4	This would be very important
DK	I don't know if this is done by our family	DK	I don't know if this will be important to our family in the future

advising and consulting with wealthy and enterprising families have validated them.

When family member participants log in to the index, they will find the behavioral practices randomized rather than arranged by category so each practice can be evaluated on its own. Participants are asked to respond to each of the behavioral practices using a rating scale of 0 to 4 (see Table 6.2), representing both the degree to which the family is currently engaging in each practice and the perception of how important the practice will be to the family's vision of sustainability in the future.

The Index is structured so that individual family members can:

- Participate online, all the while remaining anonymous, and express their viewpoints on the many practices that lead to mastering each of the four dimensions of sustainability.
- View their perspectives against those of all other family members who choose to participate.
- Understand where there is agreement and disagreement about what their family is currently doing (noted as "current assessment" in the Index) to support sustainability, factors that set the baseline and starting point of where the family is now; and see what individual family members define as the pathway to actually achieving their vision (noted as "future importance" in the Index. (See sample items presented in Table 6.3.)
- Review and develop the behaviors that will increase the likelihood of their family enterprise becoming sustainable.

The results are viewed in real time, updating as other members of the family complete the Index. Individual participants see their own results juxtaposed against everyone else's. Once everyone has weighed

TABLE 6.3

Sustainability Index: Sample Items

Practices	Current	Future
We educate beneficiaries and trustees about trust agreements and other estate planning documents that govern the transfer of family assets.	○0 ○1 ○2 ○3 ○4 ○DK	○0 ○1 ○2 ○3 ○4 ○DK
Our family shares a vision of the future.	○0 ○1 ○2 ○3 ○4 ○DK	○0 ○1 ○2 ○3 ○4 ○DK
Family members are encourged to have a sense of gratitude for the opportunites provided by family wealth.	○0 ○1 ○2 ○3 ○4 ○DK	○0 ○1 ○2 ○3 ○4 ○DK
We have an agreed upon process in place for making important decisions.	○0 ○1 ○2 ○3 ○4 ○DK	○0 ○1 ○2 ○3 ○4 ○DK
We have clear guidelines desciribing the procedure for unbundling a family member's assets from the shared assets.	○0 ○1 ○2 ○3 ○4 ○DK	○0 ○1 ○2 ○3 ○4 ○DK

in, it is important to have family discussions so that family members can share their thinking about their own ratings and why they agreed or disagreed with others' ratings. This aspect of communication—a face-to-face discussion that includes all participants—is actually quite relevant. In large families, it can often be a challenge to impart uniform information to everyone. It is no easy task when family members do not get the same information at the same time; it is not unusual for information to be misconstrued as it gets communicated to different people at different times.

Additionally, perspectives will be shown on average across all family member responses. Points of agreement and disagreement become clear but without identifying the outliers by name.

RESULTS: SETTING THE BASE POINT FOR CREATING THE FAMILY ROADMAP

There are two main sets of results generated from the Index that contribute to setting the base point: (1) the Bird's-Eye View data presented in a dimensional view chart (see Figure 6.3) and practice area tables (see Table 6.4), and (2) the Roadmap to Sustainability data in a landscape chart discussed earlier (Figure 6.1), and the preferred route table (see Table 6.1).

The Bird's-Eye View

The Bird's-Eye View is the first round of data. By first noting where family members agree and disagree, it becomes possible to engage in

Roadmap to Sustainability

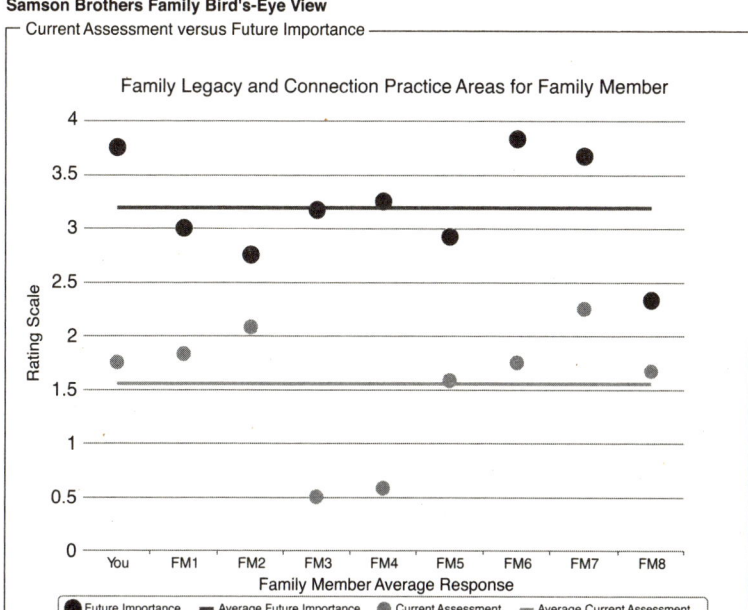

FIGURE 6.3 The Bird's-Eye View: Dimensional View

a dialogue about what actions need to be taken, if any. Where there is disagreement, opportunity exists to broaden the conversation and therefore potentially modify the way in which the family's challenges are currently being considered and managed.

As stated earlier, with each additional family member who chooses to participate, the results change to accommodate those individual perspectives and integrate them into the whole. The examples shown in the figures and tables that follow are screen shots drawn from the Family Wealth Sustainability Index results of the Samson Brothers family. While not all family members participated, nine members did, spanning the second, third, and fourth generations. Peter and his family decided that this was a representative group of the people most impacted by the family wealth and future transitions. Their results help to tell a story of what this family already believes it is doing and what it sees as important to attain future sustainability.

TABLE 6.4 The Bird's-Eye View: Practice Area Tables

The two tables below first show the "Current Assessment" followed by the "Future Importance" rating averaged across all family members for each of the practice areas within a dimension. The practice areas are defined above each of the tables and are the column labels.

Practice Areas

(1) Formulate a clear and compelling family direction

(2) Appreciate and enjoy extended family connection

(3) Develop paths for family communication

(4) Develop family's community and social mission

I. Family Legacy & Connection — Current Assessment				
Practice Areas	1	2	3	4
You	1.00	2.00	2.33	1.67
Family Member 1	2.00	2.33	2.00	1.00
Family Member 2	1.67	3.00	2.00	1.67
Family Member 3	1.33	0.67	0.00	0.00
Family Member 4	0.00	0.33	0.67	1.33
Family Member 5	0.67	1.33	2.67	1.67
Family Member 6	1.33	2.00	2.00	1.67
Family Member 7	1.33	3.00	1.67	3.00
Family Member 8	0.33	2.33	2.00	2.00

Practice Areas

(1) Formulate a clear and compelling family direction

(2) Appreciate and enjoy extended family connection

(3) Develop paths for family communication

(4) Develop family's community and social mission

I. Family Legacy & Connection — Future Importance				
Practice Areas	1	2	3	4
You	4.00	4.00	4.00	3.00
Family Member 1	3.67	2.67	3.67	2.00
Family Member 2	3.00	2.67	2.67	2.67
Family Member 3	4.00	3.00	2.67	3.00
Family Member 4	4.00	3.00	3.67	2.33
Family Member 5	3.67	2.33	4.00	1.67
Family Member 6	4.00	3.67	4.00	3.67
Family Member 7	4.00	3.33	3.67	3.67
Family Member 8	1.00	1.67	3.33	3.33

The Bird's-Eye View is composed of two main sets of results:

1. The dimensional view shows the current assessment versus future importance ratings (averaged across all practice areas within each dimension) for each family member. This includes a visual chart (see Figure 6.3). It is a highly interactive chart in that, as viewers move their mouse over each colored dot (in this book the dots are shown in shades of gray), the actual average number is revealed. Each click on the legend below the chart will make the different series of dots appear and disappear.

   For those who would prefer a text alternative to the current assessment versus future importance data, the small table simply showing the dimension heading (Table 6.5) shows the numerical values for each of the family member participants depicted in the dimensional view chart, averaged across all the practice areas. (These data can be tracked for each of the four dimensions for each family member.)

2. The practice area tables include each family member's view of the practice areas, first for current assessment and then for future importance (averaged across the behavioral practices within each practice area (see Table 6.4).

TABLE 6.5 Dimensional View (Averages)
The Dimensional View: Data table shows the data as depicted in the Birds-Eye View: The Dimensional View.
Dimensional View: Data

	I. Family Legacy & Connection	
	Current Assessment	Future Importance
Your	1.75	3.75
FM1	1.83	3.00
FM2	2.08	2.75
FM3	0.50	3.17
FM4	0.58	3.25
FM5	1.58	2.92
FM6	1.75	3.83
FM7	2.25	3.67
FM8	1.67	2.33

The Dimensional View The dimensional view is the best way to assess alignment among family members across all practice areas within a dimension. It is also a good way to establish, in general, how well family members currently perceive the family is doing on the road to sustainability and what they believe will be important in the future.

> Current Assessment rating averages equal to or greater than 3 represent a viewpoint that, at least most of the time, the family practices sustainable behavior(s) within a dimension. Future Importance ratings equal to or greater than 3 represent a viewpoint that, in order to achieve wealth sustainability, it would be solidly important for the family to practice the behavior(s) within a dimension.

Rating averages in this view show at a glance what the family perceives to be its strong suit, on the one hand, while also revealing its area in need of improvement, on the other hand. This visual chart shown in Figure 6.3 answers questions such as:

- Which dimension shows the most alignment among family members? The least?
- Which dimensions show the family agreeing it currently practices its behaviors "most of the time" (rating is equal to or greater than 3)? Or, say, "some of the time" (rating is equal to or greater than 2)?
- Which dimensions show the family agreeing "it would be solidly important in the future to practice the behaviors that define it" (rating is equal to or greater than 3)? Or, say, "moderately important" (rating is equal to or greater than 2)?

For example, in Figure 6.3, you can see that one family member is an outlier when it comes to rating how important the practices of Family Legacy and Connection are for future sustainability. That person's viewpoint is almost midway between "moderately important" and "solidly important." Additionally, given that this same family member did not view this dimension on the whole as a strong suit of the family's, what is really going on? These results might be an effective tool in promoting some candid conversations that could have been difficult otherwise.

It is already clear that there are two family members who believe the practices are currently close to "not practiced at all," with the majority of family members weighing in at "our family does this rarely." Surely, this family might want to think about whether it wants to better promote the following practice areas in its roadmap for sustainability.

- Formulate a clear and compelling family direction
- Appreciate and enjoy extended family connection
- Develop paths for family communication
- Develop family's community and social mission

Additionally, users also see where their own perceptions do or do not align with other family member perceptions. Seeing this from the vantage point of the individual user (labeled "You") allows individuals to see where they stand in relation to the other family members who participated.

The Practice Area Tables The practice area tables are the second part of the Bird's-Eye View and show the behavior practice areas that define each dimension (see Table 6.4). These tables provide more specific information about how each participant family member perceives the family's behavior in each practice area within each dimension, today and in the future. These two tables together answer questions such as:

- For each practice area, are family members more or less aligned?
- Are there outliers, family members who seem to really disagree with all the other members of the family? Taking this a step further, what might be the cause of this?
- Did you or other family members believe that all the practice areas are currently operational within your family with the same frequency? Or are some practiced more or less than others? Which ones?
- Did you or other family members believe some practice areas are more important to the family's future than others within a dimension? Which ones?

The success of a family's Roadmap to Sustainability depends on family enterprise members understanding their current situation, which is shown in the charts and tables under the heading "Bird's-Eye View." It shows where members already practice behaviors that support achieving family wealth sustainability, and where they might improve. In our work with families, we have heard over and over again the desire to have more information about what they ought to be doing to help their families have long-term success. The next section is devoted to how to understand and utilize the Roadmap to Sustainability: Landscape Chart, and the Roadmap to Sustainability: Preferred Route.

The Roadmap to Sustainability: The Landscape Chart

The landscape chart (Figure 6.1) is the first part of the second set of results that contribute to the setting of the baseline. Think about this chart providing an overview of the journey much like a set of travel directions that show the distance between each destination point along the way. While each of the practice areas are plotted within the four quadrants of this chart, the gap rating shown by the formula below is a way to estimate the distance between the base point for each practice and how far the family has to go to master the particular practice area, or how important the family views the practice area's relationship to its vision of sustainability.

The landscape chart is calculated through the formula below:

Future Importance Rating − Current Assessment Rating = Gap Rating

The *current assessment* average ratings for each practice area within a dimension are subtracted from the *future importance* average ratings to arrive at the *gap rating*.

Notice that the gap rating is the horizontal axis and the future importance rating is the vertical axis. For participating family members, when the mouse is scrolled over any of the dots, the name of the practice area, the average importance rating, and the gap score are revealed. Each dot is color coded online (and gray-shaded in this book) according to the dimension it emanates from.

Enterprising families need to be ready for and anticipate the opportunities, challenges, and inevitable changes that the future will bring.

Knowing what practices are working and which need fixing will support the family's quest for wealth sustainability.

The following points are keys to understanding the meaning of the four quadrants of the landscape chart:

- The practices that fall into the upper left quadrant—Hi Importance/Lo Gap—are the practice areas that are very important but most likely are already being practiced by the family to some degree. Sometimes, these can be a good starting point in that improvement will not be too difficult and could assist greatly in building trust and confidence in family members.
- The practices that fall into the lower left quadrant—Lo Importance/Lo Gap—are not considered very important, if at all, to the journey.
- The roadblocks to achieving family wealth sustainability primarily fall into the upper right quadrant: Hi Importance/Hi Gap.
- The practices that fall into the lower right hand quadrant—Lo Importance/Hi Gap—need attention, but secondarily.

Figure 6.1, the Roadmap to Sustainability: Landscape Chart, reveals that, on average, the Samson Brothers family members view two practice areas within Dimension I, Family Legacy and Connection, as behaviors they currently practice "well enough" or consider much less relevant to what they view as essentially important to achieving their family's wealth sustainability. However, there is one practice area within this same dimension that they view as critical, "Formulate a clear and compelling direction," which appears in the upper right quadrant—the Hi Importance/Hi Gap section—of this same chart.

In this instance, it might be fairly easy to define a starting point. Although it is not the practice area with the largest gap, it does represent the viewpoint, of all the family members combined, of what will be the most important if the family desires to achieve family wealth sustainability. But it is more difficult to discern in this chart what else the family will need to include as it plots its roadmap. For this purpose, it is useful to use the Roadmap to Sustainability: Preferred Route shown in Table 6.1.

Think about this table as identifying the most important stopovers in rank order that will define the family's Roadmap to Sustainability. By identifying the most important stopovers, the family accomplishes the first rung, "Assessing Family Sustainability," on their Roadmap

Timetable (Figure 6.2). The next steps are to establish the objectives based on the assessment, moving from the rung titled "Establish a Timeline" to "Implement a Process," which will engage family members in improving or fixing the practice areas identified by the preferred route table. The process of family members working together to achieve a common goal can serve as a laboratory for developing the family's human capital, and at the same time, can improve how the family enterprise will manage its financial capital.

While the index can help you and your family assess your current sustainability and lay out the practice areas that comprise your family's Roadmap to Sustainability, each of the chapters in this manual can assist you in a deeper understanding of each dimension, the practices that define it and how to create the objectives that will lead to your vision of sustainability. Through the case study and the examples, you can learn about what a process might look like to help you get to where you want to go.

As discussed in Chapter 2, "Family Legacy and Connection," defining a shared legacy is not as easy as it sounds. It has to do with sharing a common culture that evolves over time to incorporate the values, vision of the future, and purpose/mission of each new generation while building on the generations before. This legacy embodies both the direction of the family's holdings and the conduct of its members. The Samson Brothers family identified "formulate a clear and compelling direction" as their first-choice practice area to improve. This practice area incorporates the following behavioral practices:

- Our family mission describes our purpose.
- Values for the family are clearly articulated.
- Our family has developed a strategic plan for how the family will achieve its mission over generations.
- Our family shares a vision of the future.

The Samson Brothers Family's Unique Roadmap to Sustainability So what does this mean for the Samson Brothers as family members begin to chart a course (see Appendix 2)? Not unlike other wealthy family enterprises, they are grappling with the complexity that comes from a growing family, with a growing shared economy. They are reaping the benefits of shared opportunities while also needing to balance this with their shared risk. Additionally, they are faced with the increasing challenge of staying connected. The family experienced the consequences of Conrad's divorce from his first wife Paula, who was very close to

Emmett and his wife Jane. The next generation created their own families, increasing the branches of the family from two to four. Then Conrad re-married and Jane died. With each family change, staying connected as a family became more difficult. The brother's families had always been close, and as the composition of the family changed, they struggled with the new reality of their family dynamic.

Family enterprises do not stay static. While these structural changes were occurring within the family, the enterprise became more complex. Third-generation family members started and continued to make their careers working within the family's business and in managing growing non–real estate investments. Factors in the external environment impacted growth, positively and negatively at different times, in the cycle of the business. All the while, a fourth generation was maturing and wondering what opportunities would be open to them in the enterprise.

Without having a shared sense of a clear and compelling direction based on a mission, values, and vision, it will be difficult for these family members to have enough of an emotional and cultural connection to bond with each other. If the family does not indicate this as a current practice, then no matter what the results show, the family ought to revisit its base point results and reconsider its inclusion in their Roadmap to Sustainability. Improving or fixing this practice is foundational.

As a result of defining its future together, the family enterprise will have the tools necessary to tackle the other necessary tasks, such as defining policies regarding employment, liquidity options, exiting employment or unbundling an individual family member's assets, oversight of family financial management, and development of a responsible, self-directed next generation. It is a long list and gets longer as the complexity of the family enterprise increases—in family members, portfolio of assets, and ownership structures.

By clicking on each practice area, the highlights of each will be revealed. For the Samson Brothers family, the next stop will be to "define clear liquidity and exit options." This practice area is based on five significant behavioral practices:

1. Opt-out opportunities from participation in asset sharing are provided to individual family members.
2. We have clear policies that govern the issuance of loans or other benefits to family members.

3. An investment policy exists to meet shareholders' expected short- and long-term returns.
4. We have clear guidelines describing the procedure for unbundling a family member's assets from the shared assets.
5. In our family, when a family member chooses to remove assets from the shared family pool, their membership in the family does not change.

In the Samson Brothers family, as in many families, the situation gets complicated. Three members of the next generation and one married-in member currently work in the family enterprise. However, all the cousins will share ownership. Without the freedom for the current and future cousins to choose their own destinies, achieving wealth sustainability will be hampered. This may not be an isolated challenge the Samson Brothers family faces, but it is a challenge that poses a threat to where they are now as a family and where they want to head in the future. It is not atypical for a family such as the Samson Brothers to want access to liquidity by the third generation.

Putting It All Together   Every wealthy enterprising family can benefit from participating in the Family Wealth Sustainability Index. The information gleaned takes into account all the participating family member voices so that when the family sets out to design its unique roadmap, the base point will be more objective and concrete than assumptive.

While the roadmap provides a summary of how family members on average have chimed in with their perceptions of where the family is and what they need to do in the future, there may be more variability among family member viewpoints than shown through this particular summary. A comprehensive summary is a combination of the actions laid out by the Preferred Route table and the variability among family member perceptions as displayed in the Bird's-Eye View data.

By looking at family member perceptions by practice area in the tables (Table 6.4) you can see that family members' perceptions are more or less aligned within different practices while not in others. Given that some family members work in the enterprise and others don't, is there a different knowledge and skill base that exists among family members to account for the lack of alignment between family member perceptions? Have some members discussed liquidity and exit options and others never considered it?

Establishing a prioritized list of stopovers will not go far unless family members commit to participate. As the family clan increases in size, geographic distance, different branch cultures, family politics and dynamics, and so forth—everything becomes more intensified. For instance, engaging family members becomes more difficult. They often have a hard time understanding how they can contribute or influence decisions. And further, wealthy family enterprises often have many advisors that can direct as well as provide products and services that provide oversight and management of the family's assets. The danger lies in family members becoming complacent about their responsibility to oversee the evolving structure, legacy, and the assets placed in their stewardship and therefore, rather than fully participate in the journey, they depend on others to get them there.

THE ROADMAP TO SUSTAINABILITY: PLANNING THE FUTURE

Let's revisit the Samson Brothers family planning sessions mentioned earlier in this chapter. Once the stopover practice areas on the Roadmap to Sustainability are laid out in an orderly fashion, the family will need to devise a plan for organizing its journey. Do they need a steering committee or a family council to champion the execution of their roadmap? Will they want to think of small groups taking on responsibility for ensuring that each destination on their roadmap is fully realized? Will they need to enlist the help of nonfamily member experts to assist them on some things and not others? Will members of the family need specific preparation and education in order to fully appreciate a destination? Over what time period can they expect to see progress? How will they know they have mastered one practice area stopover and can move onto the next? These are also questions you and your family can discuss as you are pulling your own roadmap together.

The Samson family's success in attaining sustainability will depend upon its members doing the work themselves—it is in doing the work that they will gain ownership of the end result. It does not mean that they don't engage outside help, but it does mean that the work is not done by the outsider and simply delivered to them.

Each generation will also need to manage the tension between how connected and how separate they are in regard to family relationships in order to be successful at achieving sustainability. It will demand their active participation and a shift in mindset; planning for the future means planning strategically for how the whole and its branches will function. They also will need to recognize that while they share risk, they also share opportunity.

Aristotle said, "The whole is considered greater than the sum of its parts." Family members need to embrace the attitude that the interests of the family clan are more important than their own, while also maintaining a sense of self. Not an easy balance to reach. Stewardship and leadership will depend on developing this capability; otherwise the family could morph into nothing more than a group of related individuals each with his or her own agenda.

We at Relative Solutions look forward to hearing about your experiences with *The Family Wealth Sustainability Toolkit*. Please let us know on our Facebook page (www.facebook.com/RelatvSolutions) or follow us on Twitter at https://twitter.com/RelatvSolutions. As more families participate, we will update the kit to include benchmarking so you can see where your family is on the journey compared to others.

APPENDIX 1

Genogram Key

A basic family genogram includes:

Male	☐	Deceased	⊠
Female	○	Deceased	⊗

Marriage (Husband on left, Wife on right)	☐—○
Children (listed in birth order beginning on left with oldest) — **First Child** (daughter)	☐—○ with ○ child
Children — **Second Child** (son)	☐—○ with ○ and ☐ children
Living together or common-law relationships	☐- - -○
Marital separation	☐—/—○
Divorce	☐—//—○
Miscarriage	☐—○ with △
Twin children	☐—○ with ○○
Adoptions or foster children	☐—○ with ○ ☐ (dashed)
Pregnancy	☐—○ with △
Abortion	☐—○ with △ (A)

95

APPENDIX 2
The Samson Brothers Family Genograms

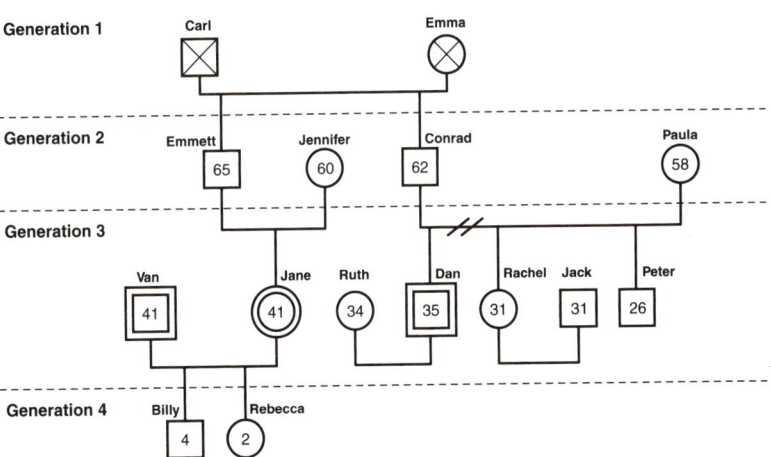

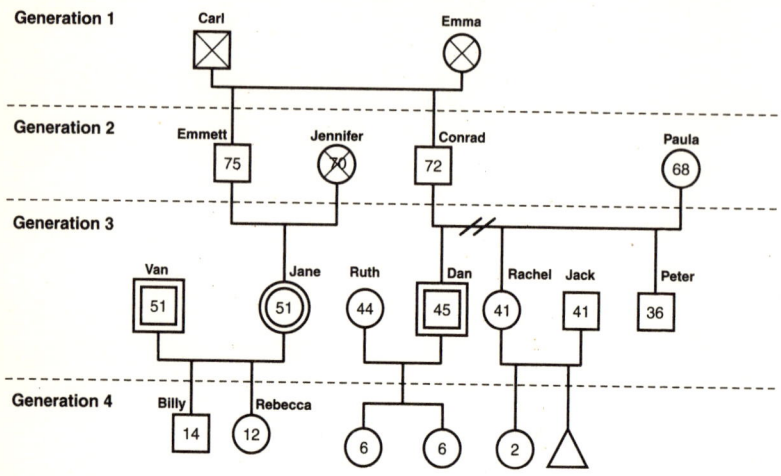

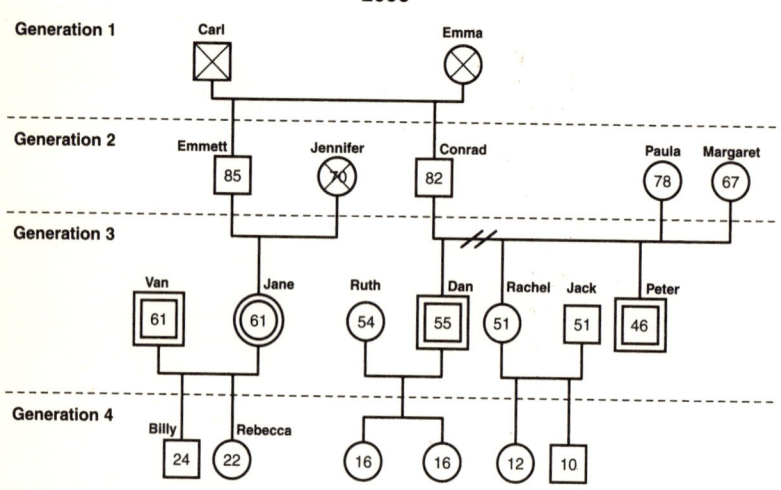

Index

A
Adulthood, transition to, 14–15
Advisers, outside, 56, 57
Advisory boards, 41
Alliances, family, 16, 17
Aristotle, 95
Assemblies, 12, 25, 44
Assets:
   growth of, 50
   in human capital, 62
   illiquid, 36
   liquid, 36, 41
   reports on, 51
   sharing, 1–2, 26. *See also* Governance structures and processes

B
Banks, family, 55
Best practices, 80, 81
Bird's-Eye View, 82, 84–88
   dimensional view, 86–88
   practice area tables, 88–89
Boards of directors, 41, 68
Bonds, shared, 26
Boundaries:
   of enterprising families, 8–10
   and governance structures, 41
Boyatzis, Richard, 64
Branch families, 13–14
Brundtland, Gro, 2, 79
Business plans, 67

C
Children, 52, 70
Codes of conduct, 67
Collective goals, personal vs., 40
Collective investor mindset, 24

Committee(s):
   education, 25
   investment, 41
Communication, family, 16–17, 43
Community involvement, 25
Competencies, relationship-based, 63–69
Complexity of connections, 26–30
Conflict resolution, 66
Conflict surfacing, 66
Constitution, family, 43–44, 67
Consultants, outside, 53–54
Continuity, fostering, 25
Culture (of family enterprises), 22
Current assessment rating averages, 87, 89

D
Decision-making processes, 36–37, 42, 45
Development, *see* Human capital and leadership development
Dimensional view, 86–88
Diversification, 67
Documents, 51

E
Economies of scale, 38
Education:
   as area for governance, 36
   and sustainability, 71–72
   of younger family members, 54
Educational messages, 53
Education committee, 25
Elder family members, 37, 38
Emotional history, shared, 5–8
Emotional intelligence, 64–65

Enterprising families, 1–19
  boundaries of, 8–10
  business of, 3–5
  creating sustainability for, 19
  definition of, 4–5
  membership challenges with, 10–13
  "public" dynamics of, 17–19
  shared emotional history of, 5–8
  transitions in, 13–15
  triangulation in, 15–17
Entitlement, sense of, 52, 67
Entrepreneurialism, 23
EQ, 65
Exploratory business ventures, 37
External visibility, 68

F
Family banks, 55
Family constitution, 43–44, 67
Family councils, 41, 45–46, 66–68, 70
Family dynamics, "public," 17–19
Family Enterprise Leadership System (FELS), 64, 65
Family history, 18
Family legacy and connection, 9–10, 19, 21–34
  case study, 31–33
  and complexity of connections, 26–30
  components of, 21
  as culture of family enterprises, 22
  other than via shared assets, 30
  philanthropy included in, ix
  and shared risk/opportunity, 22–26
Family meetings, 15, 40, 44
Family mission, 39–42
Family offices, 57
Family relationships:
  developing, 36
  dynamics of, 23
"Family think," 6
Family Wealth Sustainability Index, 2–3, 45, 75, 80–83
  benefit of using, 93
  and development of unique roadmap, 77, 78
  goal of, 42
  and next generation, 64

Financial accountability and management, 19, 49–60
  case study, 58–60
  individual's role in oversight of, 50–52
  and instilling financial responsibility, 52–55
  and long-term risk, 56–58
Financial responsibility, instilling, 52–55
Flexibility, and family connection, 26
Future, planning for the, 94–95
Future importance, 89

G
Gap rating, 89
Generational dynamics, 28, 37–38, 52
Genograms, 7–8, 97, 99–100
Getting together, 4
Goals, 39–40, 42
Goleman, Daniel, 64
Governance structures and processes, 19, 23–24, 35–48
  areas of, 36
  case study, 46–48
  development of, 42–46
  effectiveness of, 38
  and family mission, 39–42
  focus of, 39
  formalizing, 36–38
  forms of, 41
  need for, 37
Gratitude, 67
Growth:
  of family assets, 50
  long-term focus on, 23
  in number of family members, 23

H
Human capital and leadership development, 19, 25, 61–74
  case study, 72–74
  definition of human capital, 62
  philanthropy included in, ix
  as process, 62–63
  and relationship-based competencies, 63–69
  value of, 69–72

I

Illiquid assets, 36
Information, sharing, 53
In-laws, membership challenges for, 11–12
Investing (financial), 54
Investment (in family members), 22–23
Investment committees, 41

J

Joint ownership, 55

L

Landscape chart, 76, 89–91
Lao Tzu, 68
Leaders, family, 65, 68–69
Leadership development, *see* Human capital and leadership development
"Leading by example," 70
Legacy, family, *see* Family legacy and connection
Limited liability corporations, 51
Liquid assets, 36, 41
Lombardi, Vince, 63
Long-term focus, 23
Long-term risk and finance management, 56–58

M

"Making your mark," 26–28
Managers, outside, 56–57
Market share, decline in, 24
Marriage, 10–11, 13, 28–29
Mayer, John D., 64–65
McKee, Annie, 64
Medical policies, 13–14
Meetings, family, 15, 40, 44
Membership:
  challenges of, 10–13
  ownership vs., 30
Mentors, 71
Mission, family, 39–42
Money:
  differing values toward, 37
  and wealth, 61

N

Newcomers, family, 28–29

O

Offices, family, 57
Opportunity, shared, 24–26
Opting out, 44
Orientation for new members, 12–13
Our Common Future (UN report), 79
Outside help, getting, 53–54, 56–57
Ownership:
  joint, 55
  membership vs., 30
  sense of shared, 53–54
  stewardship vs., 50–51

P

Past, influence of the, 7
Patriarchs, 38
"Personal bucket," 55
Personal goals, collective vs., 40
Philanthropy, ix, 25, 26, 36, 54, 66
Planning for the future, 94–95
Polarization, 15
Practice area tables, 88–89
Preferred Route, 76, 77, 82, 89–91, 93
Prenuptial agreements, 11
Primal Leadership (Goleman, Boyatzis, and McKee), 64
"Public" family dynamics, 17–19
Public information, 53

R

Raison d'être, 39
Regeneration of wealth, 50
Relationship-based competencies, 63–69
Relationships, as family energy source, 62
Relative Solutions, 2, 64, 95
Reports, on financial assets, 51
Responsibility, financial, 52–55
Retirement, of senior leaders, 13
Return on investment (ROI), 50
Risk:
  best hedge against, 50
  long-term, 56–58
  shared, 23–24

Roadmap Timetable, 77, 78, 90
Roadmap to sustainability, 75–95
   Bird's-Eye View, 82, 84–88
   case study, 79–80, 91–95
   designing your, 77–79
   dimensional view, 86–88
   and Family Wealth Sustainability Index, 80–83
   landscape chart, 76, 89–91
   and planning for the future, 94–95
   practice area tables, 88–89
   setting base point for, 82–94
   timetable for developing, 78
Rockefeller family, 25

S
Salovey, Peter, 64–65
Samson Brothers Family case study, 30
   family legacy and connection, 31–33
   financial accountability and management, 58–60
   genograms, 99–100
   governance structures and processes, 46–48
   human capital and leadership development, 72–74
   roadmap to sustainability, 79–80, 91–95
Self-worth, 25
Senior leaders, retirement of, 13
Sense of purpose, shared, 36
Separateness, 9, 26, 30
Shared assets, 26, 30, 35, 53
Shared bonds, 26
Shared economy, 50
Shared emotional history, 5–8
Shared information, 53
Shared ownership, sense of, 53–54
Shared risk and opportunity, 22–26
Social mission, shared, 25–26
Staying together, 4
Stewardship, 51
Stopovers, 76
Strategic planning, 69–70
Succession planning, 63
Suspiciousness, 10

Sustainability:
   best practices for, 80, 81
   concept of, ix
   difficulty of achieving, 21
   dimensions of, x. *See also individual dimensions*
   for enterprising families, 19
   as evolutionary process, 5
   goal of, 52
Sustainability Index, *see* Family Wealth Sustainability Index

T
Teams, and shared bonds, 26
Tension(s):
   marriage and, 29
   triangulation and, 16
Transitions, 13–15, 39
Transparency, 43, 53
Triangulation, 15–17
Trust:
   creating, 23, 42
   importance of, 58
Trusts, 56
Trustees, 56–57

U
Uniqueness, each family's, 40
United Nations World Commission on Environment and Development (WCED), 2

V
Visibility, external, 68
Vision, 25

W
Wealth:
   growing family, 50
   money vs., 61
   regeneration of, 50
   and transition to adulthood, 14–15

Y
Younger family members, 37, 54
   and conflict resolution, 66
   and trustees, 56–57

Stay in touch!

Subscribe to our free Finance and Accounting eNewsletters at
www.wiley.com/enewsletters

Visit our blog: **www.capitalexchangeblog.com**

Follow us on Twitter
@wiley_finance

"Like" us on Facebook
www.facebook.com/wileyglobalfinance

Find us on LinkedIn
Wiley Global Finance Group

WILEY Global Finance
WHERE DATA FINDS DIRECTION